THE LOVE OF
LONDON

THE LOVE OF
LONDON

Wilfrid Rolfe

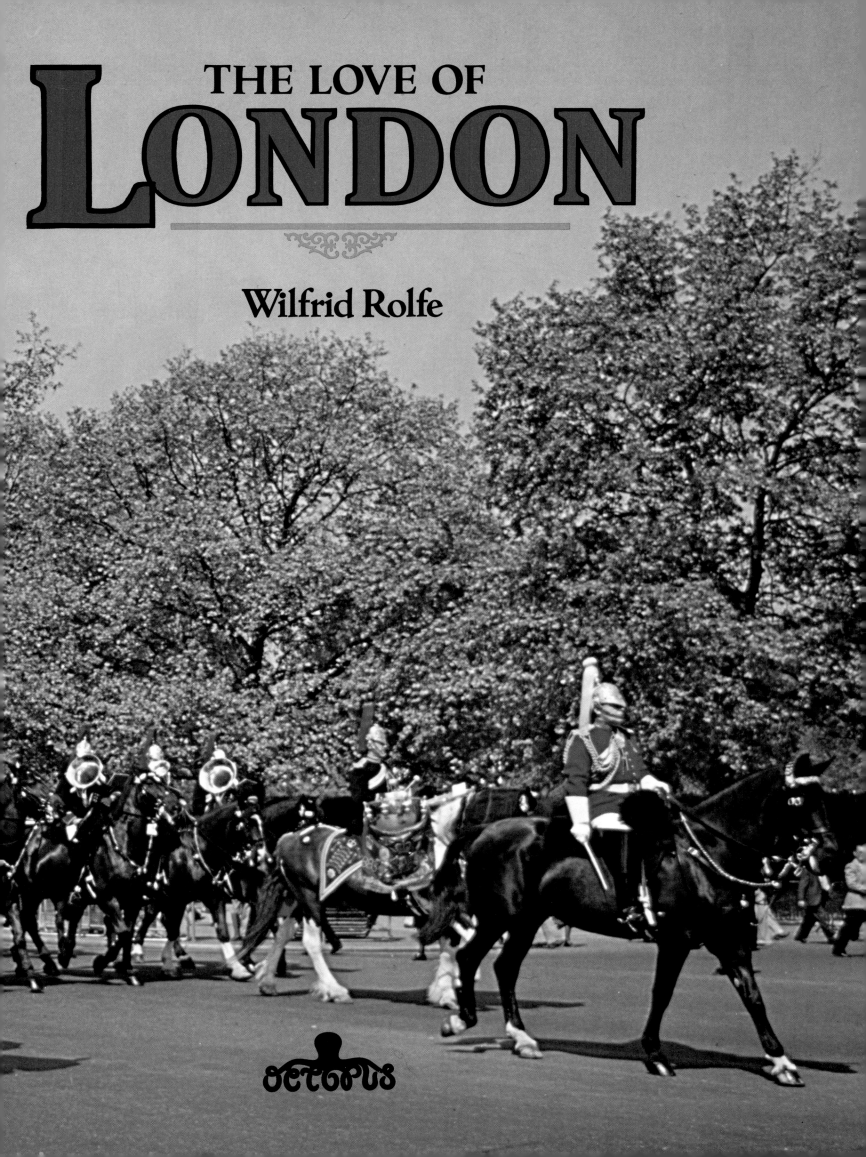

octopus

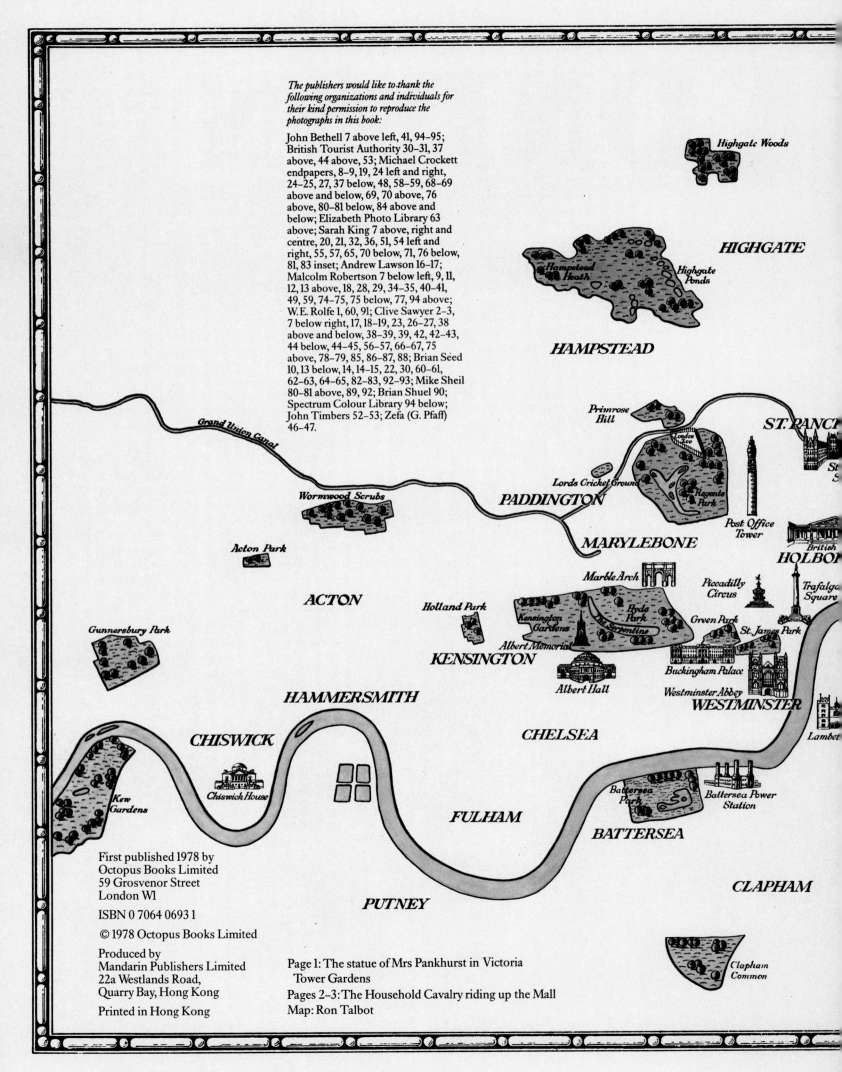

The publishers would like to thank the
following organizations and individuals for
their kind permission to reproduce the
photographs in this book:

John Bethell 7 above left, 41, 94–95;
British Tourist Authority 30–31, 37
above, 44 above, 53; Michael Crockett
endpapers, 8–9, 19, 24 left and right,
24–25, 27, 37 below, 48, 58–59, 68–69
above and below, 69, 70 above, 76
above, 80–81 below, 84 above and
below; Elizabeth Photo Library 63
above; Sarah King 7 above, right and
centre, 20, 21, 32, 36, 51, 54 left and
right, 55, 57, 65, 70 below, 71, 76 below,
81, 83 inset; Andrew Lawson 16–17;
Malcolm Robertson 7 below left, 9, 11,
12, 13 above, 18, 28, 29, 34–35, 40–41,
49, 59, 74–75, 75 below, 77, 94 above;
W.E. Rolfe 1, 60, 91; Clive Sawyer 2–3,
7 below right, 17, 18–19, 23, 26–27, 38
above and below, 38–39, 39, 42, 42–43,
44 below, 44–45, 56–57, 66–67, 75
above, 78–79, 85, 86–87, 88; Brian Seed
10, 13 below, 14, 14–15, 22, 30, 60–61,
62–63, 64–65, 82–83, 92–93; Mike Sheil
80–81 above, 89, 92; Brian Shuel 90;
Spectrum Colour Library 94 below;
John Timbers 52–53; Zefa (G. Pfaff)
46–47.

Highgate Woods

HIGHGATE

Hampstead Heath

Highgate Ponds

HAMPSTEAD

Grand Union Canal

Primrose Hill

ST. PANCI

London Zoo

Lords Cricket Ground

Regents Park

PADDINGTON

Wormwood Scrubs

Post Office Tower

British

HOLBOR

MARYLEBONE

Acton Park

Marble Arch

Piccadilly Circus

Trafalga Square

ACTON

Holland Park

Kensington Gardens

Hyde Park

The Serpentine

Green Park

St. James Park

Gunnersbury Park

Albert Memorial

Buckingham Palace

KENSINGTON

Albert Hall

Westminster Abbey

WESTMINSTER

HAMMERSMITH

Lambet

CHISWICK

CHELSEA

Chiswick House

Battersea Park

Battersea Power Station

Kew Gardens

FULHAM

BATTERSEA

CLAPHAM

First published 1978 by
Octopus Books Limited
59 Grosvenor Street
London W1

ISBN 0 7064 0693 1

© 1978 Octopus Books Limited

Produced by
Mandarin Publishers Limited
22a Westlands Road,
Quarry Bay, Hong Kong

Printed in Hong Kong

PUTNEY

Clapham Common

Page 1: The statue of Mrs Pankhurst in Victoria
Tower Gardens
Pages 2–3: The Household Cavalry riding up the Mall
Map: Ron Talbot

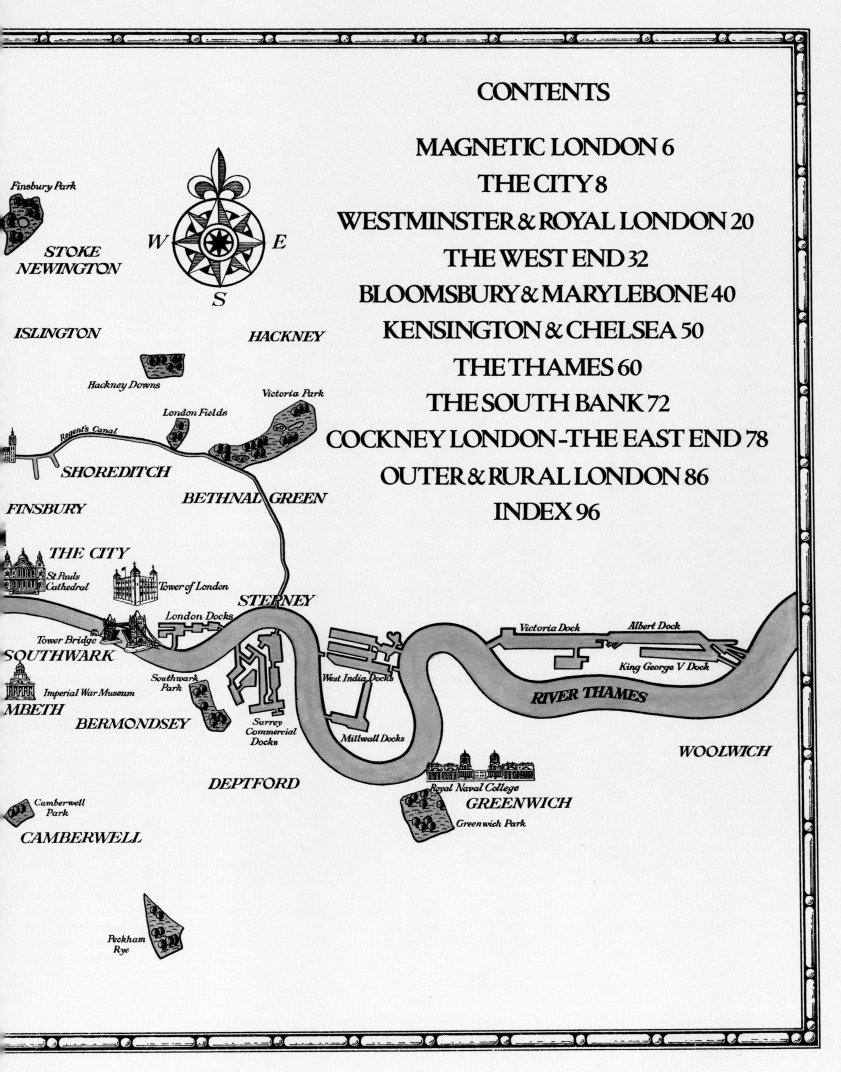

CONTENTS

Finsbury Park

STOKE
NEWINGTON

W E
S

ISLINGTON

HACKNEY

Hackney Downs

Victoria Park

London Fields

Regent's Canal

SHOREDITCH

BETHNAL GREEN

FINSBURY

THE CITY

St. Pauls Cathedral

Tower of London

STEPNEY

London Docks

Tower Bridge

SOUTHWARK

MBETH

Imperial War Museum

Southwark Park

BERMONDSEY

Surrey Commercial Docks

West India Docks

Millwall Docks

Victoria Dock

Albert Dock

King George V Dock

RIVER THAMES

WOOLWICH

DEPTFORD

Camberwell Park

Royal Naval College

GREENWICH

Greenwich Park

CAMBERWELL

Peckham Rye

MAGNETIC LONDON

No one can satisfactorily explain personal magnetism. As Sir James Barrie said of charm: 'It's a sort of bloom on a woman. If you have it you don't need to have anything else; and if you don't have it, it doesn't matter what else you have.'

Anyone who doubts the personal magnetism of London should join the thousands who make the morning pilgrimage to Buckingham Palace to watch the Changing of the Guard or who constantly queue at the Tower of London to get a glimpse of the Crown Jewels. Where royalty and pageantry combine London's magnetism is at its most powerful.

But the attractions of London in more specialized ways are just as strong. London's shops draw in their customers not only from the most distant parts of Britain but also from half the countries of the world. The London theatre has an unchallenged reputation. Though London is reticent about its treasures, its art galleries and museums house more of the world's great artistic masterpieces than Paris or Rome. Palaces, cathedrals, churches, historic buildings, parks, concert halls: London provides a richness of choice which leaves the receptive visitor – and even the grateful resident – gasping. In addition there are in London, for those who seek them, haunts 'where the busy world is hushed': an alley off some city street leading to a secret garden; a square cool with plane trees, those uncomplaining providers of London shade; a deck chair beside a park lake where the only sound is the quacking of bright-eyed ducks; the heart-lifting glow of a London sunset seen from a boat on the Serpentine. No wonder that Londoners, however far they may be from home, look to this city with all its varied attractions as the centre of their world.

For those who do, this book may well nourish their nostalgia rather than cure it. The pictures will inevitably rekindle happy memories while the text may, perhaps, shed new light on familiar scenes. But for those to whom London is merely a name, the book has a more definite purpose. Bricks and mortar are meaningless sights unless the people and events connected with them are known. That is why the text does its best to add an historical perspective to the pictures; to give them meaning beyond their pictorial attractions.

For the visitor to London this is no substitute for a guide book though it might be said to be the nicest souvenir. If it communicates something of the magnetism that London exudes it will have done a major part of its job.

London's magnetism is nothing new. More than two thousand years ago the Early Britons were attracted to the site and established a settlement on the north bank of the Thames at the mouth of the Wallbrook, where Cannon Street station stands today.

The site's advantages were self-evident: it was above the level of the nearby marshes, was defended on the west by the river Fleet and to the south by the broad natural moat of the Thames. It lay in the centre of the island's most populous and fertile region and a fine broad tideway gave the rapidly developing trade of the country easy access to the continent of Europe. Upstream the sinuous Thames wound its way through the expanding heart of England. As the site for the country's principal city it seemed then, as it seems today, the inevitable choice.

When the Romans colonized the country in the middle of the first century AD, they had established their administrative base at Camulodunum in Essex, now known as Colchester. They soon discovered their mistake and by 61 AD the move to London was under way. One of their first actions was to build a wall around the city to defend it against land attack. By building a 6 m (20 ft) high wall of Kentish ragstone and Roman tiles they set the limits of the city for the next thousand years. It seems probable that the Emperor Hadrian, builder of the famous 130 km (80 mile) wall across the north of England from Wallsend to Solway Firth, was also responsible for the first permanent defences of London. So permanent were they that portions of the wall may still be seen near the Tower of London, beside the Barbican, and in St Martin's-le-Grand. But most of it has been removed and the rest incorporated in modern streets and buildings.

The Romans finally withdrew from Britain in 423 AD as a result of the Saxon invasion of south-east England. The invaders captured London which they totally destroyed – except for the wall. And when they came to build their own Saxon city on the site it was the Roman wall that still marked its limits.

The next 400 years are virtually a blank page in the history of London. The city changed hands many times until in 886 AD King Alfred defeated the Danish invaders and regained it. From then on London's role as a great trading centre went from strength to strength.

The next red-letter date in London's history was 1066 when, as everybody knows, William of Normandy invaded Britain, killed King Harold at the Battle of Hastings and – inevitably – hurried towards London where he had himself crowned William the First of England on Christmas Day. Sensing the mood of the English – hostile to put it mildly – he looked around for the safest place to live. By this time the inhabitants of London had helped themselves liberally to the stones from the Roman walls and, close to the Thames on the eastern boundary, there was a convenient and highly defensible gap. This gap William plugged with the Keep of what was later to become the Tower of London. His first home – the White Tower – stands today very nearly as William built it. It is certainly the oldest complete building in London and none is more redolent of its violent past.

Up to this time the advantages of living within the safety of the city walls were so obvious that the population of London had exploded and accommodation of all sorts was at a premium, so much so that development had spread westward beyond the walls along what is now Queen Victoria Street, Holborn and Fleet Street. Further west, and quite separate from the City of London, the City of Westminster had grown up around the abbey founded in the dark ages but rebuilt by Edward the Confessor in about 1050 AD. Nothing of this pre-Norman abbey remains and much of the present Westminster Abbey dates from the reign of Henry III by which time Westminster had become the established home of the kings of England and the centre of political power and governmental administration. Of the extensive Palace of Westminster buildings only the magnificent Westminster Hall remains. Thus the London of today has grown out of the union of two separate cities, one the seat of kings, the other a hive of commerce. Though they meet at Temple Bar, where the Strand becomes Fleet Street, they maintain to a surprising extent their separate identities, sharing only this indefinable quality: the magnetism of London

Woburn Walk, Bloomsbury, where the Georgian shopfronts with wrought iron balustrades take one straight back to the 18th century. (*Above*)
A pikeman of the Honourable Artillery Company escorting the Lord Mayor's Coach. (*Left*)
A glimpse of Shaftesbury Avenue, full of taxis and theatregoers. (*Below left*)
Part of the impressive sculptured relief which decorates the base of the Albert Memorial in Kensington Gardens. (*Below right*)
The statue of Eros in Piccadilly Circus, the traditional centre of London's West End. (*Right*)
A Thames barge passing the Royal Naval College at Greenwich in the annual barge race. (*Above right*)

THE CITY

COMMERCIAL AND FINANCIAL LONDON – 'The City' – is little more than a village in terms of population. About five thousand people are permanent residents; but another half million flood into its offices, markets, shops and warehouses each morning and retreat to their homes outside the City each night. This twice-daily migration puts a daunting strain on the railways, underground and buses and, particularly, on the barely adequate roads.

Viewed from the air the City's road system within its roughly semicircular perimeter resembles a child's early efforts at drawing. There are plenty of roads, many of them narrow, and they dart off in every direction, merging, forking, bending and doubling back on themselves – a traffic planner's nightmare. If there seems to be little logic in the layout it has to be remembered that these are streets that have grown out of Roman, Saxon and Danish streets – all streets within the walled City that was the beginning of London, streets that had nowhere to go outside the walls. Though the seven City gates that pierced the walls in medieval times are now gone, the streets that led to them still exist and are named after them: Cripplegate, Ludgate, Newgate, Aldersgate, Moorgate, Bishopsgate and Aldgate.

In medieval times there was so little wheeled traffic that the narrow streets, though filthy, were more or less adequate. Even in the late 17th century the quickest and cheapest way to travel to Westminster or Greenwich (as Samuel Pepys so often records) was not to go by coach but to walk down one of the many lanes leading to the Thames and there hire a waterman to row you. The Thames was the great east–west highway and its counterpart for the motoring age has yet to be built.

There have been two occasions when it would have been possible to replan the City's streets: the first after the Great Fire of London in 1666 and the second after the devastation of the *Blitz* during World War II. Curiously the area of damage in these two catastrophes was similar and in both cases the bold, imaginative plans for rebuilding were watered down and opportunities lost.

Sir Christopher Wren was early on the scene after the Great Fire. Almost before the embers had cooled he presented a plan which envisaged a new Royal Exchange as the centre of the City, surrounded by an extensive piazza from which wide streets radiated in all directions, two of them forming main east–west thoroughfares. Unfortunately this plan was rejected on the grounds that it involved too much redistribution of property. The only parts of his plan to survive were the rebuilding of St Paul's Cathedral and a broad quay between the Tower and the Temple (sadly built over in the 19th century). He also rebuilt many of the 87 city churches destroyed in the fire, turning London into a treasure house of ecclesiastical architecture. In addition, some streets were widened (though not to the extent that Wren advised) and many of the extremely advanced building standards he recommended to prevent future fires were adopted.

Since World War II, certain areas of the City have been redeveloped with great courage and imagination – notably the Barbican scheme and the improvement in traffic flow as a result of the widening of London Wall, but there is little outward sign of any long-term plan for the City. Happily its post-war buildings, many of them tower blocks which dwarf the 110 m (365 ft) high dome of St Pauls, make no attempt to ape the past and so encourage closer attention to the many ancient treasures that remain: St Paul's Cathedral, the Tower of London, the Guildhall, St Bartholomew-the-Great and the many city churches designed by Wren, the Inns of Court, the Royal Exchange, the Mansion House and several of the halls of the City Livery Companies.

The Bank of England is the City's centre of gravity and integrity, with six busy streets meeting at its door. The phrase 'safe as the Bank of England' still has meaning although there was the occasion when the directors of the bank received an anonymous letter stating that the writer knew a way into the bullion room. This they ignored until a second letter offered to meet them in the bullion room on any day and at any time they cared to name. The appointment was made and the directors locked themselves in to await the anonymous correspondent's arrival. He appeared right on time, forcing up some boards in the floor of the vault to make his entry. Fortunately he turned out to be an honest man employed on repairing sewers beneath the bank and he was awarded £800 for his integrity.

There need be no concern for the safety of Britain's gold reserves: the incident is said to have happened in 1836 and the bank vaults have been totally rebuilt since then. In fact the whole of the bank was rebuilt between 1921 and the outbreak of World War II. All that remains of Sir John Soane's early 19th century building is the windowless curtain wall on the south and west sides.

The headquarters of many banks and financial institutions were rebuilt in the inter-war years – not a happy period for British architecture. They were, it would seem, designed to impress the customers and to emphasize the probity of the occupants. In their black-coated, bowler-hatted way they did both, but the solidity of the 20s has become the stuffiness of the 70s and these solid, undoubtedly burglar-proof buildings have neither the adventurousness of some of the recent buildings nor the innate good taste of Wren or Soane.

ENTRY TO THE TRAITORS' GATE

THE earliest part of the Tower of London is the Keep or White Tower, here seen through trees from the opposite bank of the Thames. It was designed for William the Conqueror by Gundulf, a Benedictine monk who later became Bishop of Rochester. His instructions from William were clear: a building that would overawe the Londoners; provide a safe home for the king; and serve as a stronghold from which to crush any possible rebellion. It was completed in 1097, occupying a space where the disintegrating Roman Wall joined the Thames. The various buildings of the Tower have served as palace, prison, home of the Royal Mint, site of a Royal Menagerie and of the Royal Observatory. It still guards the Crown Jewels, and the nightly Ceremony of the Keys – the official locking of the Tower – has been carried on without a break for 700 years. (*Above*)

THE Old Rectory of St Dunstan-in-the-East. The church, gutted in the *Blitz* of 1941, was not rebuilt but its Wren tower still stands. (*Right*)

About half of the daily influx of workers into the City must cross one of the four road bridges and two rail bridges that link it with South London across the Thames. The most easily recognized of these is Tower Bridge, whose profile is almost a London trade mark. But the most used is its upstream neighbour, London Bridge. There has been a bridge here since at least the 10th century and, until 1749, old London Bridge was the only river crossing for traffic in London. The first permanent bridge was begun here in 1176 at the instigation of the rector of St Mary Colechurch, a church which was destroyed in the Great Fire and never rebuilt. The bridge, 33 years in the building, ultimately had 19 pointed stone arches, two waterwheels operated by the tide, a drawbridge at its northern end, tall blocks of shops and houses, and a chapel dedicated to Thomas à Becket. As time went by the narrow roadway became quite inadequate for the traffic wanting to cross, and the narrow arches, becoming blocked by ice, caused the Thames to freeze over in the arctic winters of 1515, 1564, 1620, 1683 and 1814. Londoners made the best of it holding fairs, ox-roastings and even a fox hunt on the frozen surface. By the end of the 18th century Old London Bridge had become such an anachronism that the *Quarterly Review* was prompted to write: 'This pernicious structure has wasted more money in perpetual repairs than would have sufficed to build a dozen safe and commodious bridges.' A new London Bridge, designed by John Rennie, was built by his son in 1831 46 m (50 yds) upstream from the old, and this bridge stood for a further 140 years, by which time it, too, had become over-congested. As the present bridge was being built, Rennie's bridge was being dismantled stone by stone and shipped to Lake Havasu City, Arizona, where it has become a popular tourist attraction.

One of London's unique institutions is the City Livery Company of which there are nearly 90 today. They evolved out of the craft guilds of the late Middle Ages. Even in those days there were industrial disputes and in London the 'masters' split away from the craftsmen members of the guilds and formed their own city companies. Over the years these companies, many of which evolved their own ceremonial dress or 'livery', devoted themselves less to the daily problems of the craft and more to charitable and educational work. The school founded by the Merchant Taylors' Company is well known, and Sir John Gresham, a member of the Mercers' Company, founded Gresham's School in his home county of Norfolk. He later became a member of the Fishmongers' Company who are still the school's trustees. Many of these city companies accumulated great wealth and were able to build handsome and luxurious Livery Halls, several of which still exist. The Fishmongers' Hall is a prominent building at the north end of London Bridge. The Goldsmiths' Hall is harder to find – in Foster Lane off Gresham Street. Here the annual Trial of the Pyx is held – a picturesque ceremony with a serious purpose: to check the accuracy of composition and weight of newly minted coinage.

Much that goes on in the City of London must look like idle ceremony to the outsider: the Lord Mayor's Show, the Honourable Artillery Company, the medieval clothing of City officials and the nightly Ceremony of the Keys at the Tower of London are all quaint in the modern context in which they are seen, but they represent a thread of continuity in the life of the great City of London which would certainly make London the poorer for their passing ✍🐦

THESE picturesquely uniformed pikemen are members of the Honourable Artillery Company, the oldest volunteer regiment in Britain. Founded as a body of archers known as the Guild of St George, it was granted a royal charter by Henry VIII in 1537 with the title of the Fraternity of Longbows, Crossbows and Handguns. Though the HAC is an active, modern army unit, it preserves its close links with royalty and the City by providing the Company of Pikemen and Musketeers – mostly the senior members of the Company – who do duty on ceremonial occasions. (*Above*)

THE City of London is administered from its historic Guildhall. Here, every year in November, the Lord Mayor's banquet is held, and here, every other Thursday, the Court of Common Council – the City's governing body – holds its meetings which are open to the public. (*Right*)

WHEN the Jewish moneylenders were banished from England in 1290, Italian merchants moved in from Lombardy to establish themselves as bankers in the City of London – in what is known today as Lombard Street. It runs from close to the Bank of England to Gracechurch Street. Here the gilded signs hang like medieval banners to indicate the presence of almost every firm of importance in the world of banking and insurance. (*Left*)

ST Paul's Cathedral has had an exciting career stretching over nearly 14 centuries. The first cathedral, founded in AD 604, was burnt; the second was vandalized by the Vikings; a third was burnt to the ground in 1087; the fourth – known as Old St Paul's – lost its steeple in a thunderstorm in 1561 and finally succumbed to the Great Fire of 1666. While the present cathedral was being built Sir Christopher Wren is said to have lived in a house, now known as Cardinal's Wharf, on the opposite bank of the Thames, from which he was able to keep a constant eye on the building's progress.
The cathedral's most prominent feature – the dome – climbs to a height of 111m (365 feet) and is 34m (112 feet) in diameter. It is carried on eight piers and is made up of a brick inner dome beneath a brick cone which supports the Baroque lantern surmounted by a golden ball and cross. The outer dome is of timber sheathed in lead. During the bombing raids of 1940 and 1941, St Paul's was the centre of an area of great destruction but, apart from damage to the High Altar, the choir stalls and the sanctuary screen, it miraculously escaped.
Many of Britain's national heroes are buried within the cathedral including Nelson and Wellington. Sir Christopher Wren's own tomb is in the crypt and bears the often quoted inscription: '*Lector, si monumentum requiris, circumspice*' – 'Reader, if you seek his monument, look around you'.
The picture shows the west front of the cathedral seen from Ludgate Hill. (*Right*)

THOUGH the streets of London may not be paved with gold, as the song once had it, vast quantities of the precious metal are stored in the vaults of the City's bullion merchants and banks. The bullion room of the Bank of England contains several hundreds of millions of pounds' worth of gold and it must be the most secure safe deposit in the whole of the United Kingdom. But London is also a great gold market and the City's merchants have to handle and transport large numbers of gold ingots both for sale to jewellery manufacturers and for export abroad. In order to keep track of the gold, each ingot is numbered and recorded. Private individuals are no longer permitted to buy, sell or hoard gold, and its use in coinage was discontinued in 1914. (*Left*)

I N a ceremony that has scarcely changed in 600
years, the Liverymen of the City of London elect
their Lord Mayor each year on 29 September,
Michaelmas Day, the Feast of St Michael and All
Angels. It takes place in the Guildhall where a
temporary barricade-like construction known as the
'Wickets' is erected across the lower frontage of the
building. Voting Liverymen of the various city
companies enter the Guildhall through their appropriate Wicket and are vetted by the attendant
Beadles, ready to eject any gatecrashing intruders.
The newly elected Lord Mayor plays no further part
in City ceremonies until Admission Day, the second
Friday in November when, following a luncheon at
the Mansion House (the Lord Mayor's official
residence) he is sworn in at the Guildhall and receives
his symbols of office – the Sword and Mace, the
Crystal Sceptre, the Seal and the City Purse. The
new and the retiring Lord Mayors then exchange
seats without a word – a ceremony known as the
Silent Change. (*Above*)

O N the next day is held the Lord Mayor's Show,
a traditional procession to the Royal Courts of
Justice where the Lord Mayor makes his statutory
declaration of office to the Lord Chief Justice before
continuing along the Strand and the Victoria
Embankment through cheering crowds back to the
Mansion House. On the following Monday the Lord
Mayor's Banquet is held in Guildhall. The Prime
Minister is a guest on this occasion and usually
makes some significant political statement when
responding to the toast of Her Majesty's Ministers.
The magnificent coach in which the Lord Mayor
rides was built in 1757 and is normally to be seen in
the Guildhall Museum. For its one day of glory in
the outside world its two-and-a-half tons of elabor-
ately gilded, carved and painted coachwork are
hauled by six shire horses from the stables of
Whitbread's brewery. Beside it march the Pikemen
of the Honourable Artillery Company in their
17th century uniforms with plumed helmets and
crimson sashes. Within the coach the Lord Mayor is
dressed in the fur-trimmed scarlet robe, the Cap of
Dignity and the 16th century chain of office known
as the Lord Mayor's Collar of 'SS'. For him it is the
beginning of an exhausting year. (*Right*)

LINCOLN'S Inn, one of London's four Inns of Court – the university of the legal profession – is an oasis of calm just out of earshot of the thunderous traffic of Fleet Street and Chancery Lane. To wander through its Tudor brick gatehouse is to discover an unexpected world of manicured lawns and echoing courtyards full of narrow doorways and staircases, reminiscent of Oxford or Cambridge. (*Above*)

THE new legal year begins on 1 October and, to mark the event, a service is held in Westminster Abbey. From here, the red-robed judges and all the other dignitaries of the law form a procession to the House of Lords where they are entertained by the Lord Chancellor at what is modestly known as a 'breakfast'. (*Left*)

ANYONE who is prepared to climb 311 steps up a spiral staircase can experience this view of the modernized City of London from the top of the Monument in Fish Street Hill. The 61.6m (202 feet) high Doric column commemorates the Great Fire of 1666. The significance of its height is that it is said to stand on a spot exactly 61.6m (202 feet) from the baker's shop in Pudding Lane where the conflagration began in an oven chimney. The Monument, like so many things after the Fire, was designed by Wren. His original intention was to have gilt spikes simulating flames emerging from loop-holes up the sides of the column with a statue of Charles II on top but in the end he had to settle for no flames and an urn. This view, looking up the curve of Gracechurch Street, leads the eye to the headquarters of the National Westminster Bank – the tallest building in London. (*Right*)

OF the 87 City churches destroyed in the Great Fire of 1666, Sir Christopher Wren rebuilt 53, making London a rich repository of ecclesiastical architecture. Of the 47 still surviving at the outbreak of World War II, 20 were seriously damaged by bombing, some so seriously that only 12 of the 20 have been fully restored. One of these is a church with the rare dedication to St Vedast. It is in Foster Lane, just to the north and in sight of St Paul's. Even so eminent an architectural writer as Sir Nikolaus Pevsner finds himself lost for words in attempting to describe the light and shade effects of the Baroque steeple. The interior has been handsomely restored but is probably too bright, frigid and precise to have gained Sir Christopher's full approval. The only other church in England dedicated to St Vedast (a French saint) is at Tathwell in Lincolnshire. (*Left*)

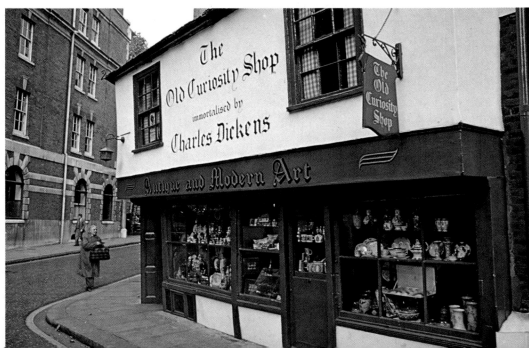

CHARLES Dickens wrote his famous story 'The Old Curiosity Shop' while he was living in Marylebone, at No. 1 Devonshire Terrace, but his book is much more closely connected in the public imagination with this 17th century building near Lincoln's Inn Fields which has latched on to the legend to its obvious benefit. How genuine the connection is is a matter for individual conjecture. E. V. Lucas's *London*, published in 1926, says that the Old Curiosity Shop 'has now passed into the hands of a firm of tailors'. A London guide published over 100 years ago fails to mention it at all. Dickens purists say that the true site of the Old Curiosity Shop is near the National Portrait Gallery where the statue of Sir Henry Irving, the famous Victorian actor, now stands. Whatever the truth, the Old Curiosity Shop is today firmly back in the curio business. (*Left*)

WESTMINSTER
& ROYAL LONDON

WESTMINSTER, THOUGH ONLY ONE OF London's thirty-two boroughs, stoutly preserves its traditional entity as a city in its own right – a city which, until building development seeped along the north bank of the Thames in the Middle Ages, was quite separate from the City of London, three km (two miles) to the east.

Today, unless you happen to be the Queen, you can pass freely between Westminster and the City 'without let or hindrance'. But the Queen is obliged to stop at Temple Bar (the City's western boundary) and indicate her intention to enter the City. The Lord Mayor of London immediately surrenders the Pearl Sword presented to the City by Queen Elizabeth I in 1571 which the Queen equally immediately returns, and Her Majesty continues on her way. This picturesque ceremony is, of course, merely a formality but it underlines the City's traditional independence without disrespect to the Crown.

Within the City of Westminster the Queen suffers no restrictions. She and her ancestors have made it their home for more than a thousand years. Ever since the early English kings dragged themselves away from their ancient capital at Winchester (it was the excellent hunting in the New Forest that kept them there so long) Westminster has enjoyed a special relationship with the Crown. Every monarch since William the Conqueror (except Edward V and Edward VIII who were never crowned) has been crowned in Westminster Abbey. Parliament has gathered there (at one time in the Abbey's chapter house) since the 10th century. Most of London's royal pageantry takes place within Westminster's boundaries. The history of these islands and its monarchy is embedded in its stones. Though Westminster in recent years has spread and absorbed the London boroughs of Marylebone and Paddington, making it in terms of rateable value richer than the City of London itself, most people think of it as the relatively compact area between the Thames and Buckingham Palace and between the Houses of Parliament and Trafalgar Square. Within this readily explorable area the imaginative visitor can enjoy two Westminsters: the imposing present day city of parks and Parliament and palaces; and the Westminster of history whose many streets and buildings link the disappearing past with the fast changing present.

The Houses of Parliament are Westminster's most prominent present day feature but adjoining them is Westminster Hall, built by William Rufus, son of the Conqueror, and re-roofed by Richard II (1377–99) with one of the most splendid hammerbeam roofs in Europe. It is the sole surviving building of the fascinating jumble that was once the extensive Palace of Westminster, destroyed in the fire of 1834. Fortunately for our imaginations both Turner and Constable rushed to the scene with their sketch pads and made vivid pictorial records of the biggest conflagration that London had seen since the Great Fire of 1666.

Halfway up Whitehall, opposite the Horse Guards, the Banqueting House reminds modern London that here, stretching from the banks of

Pubs and Palaces. London has plenty of both and here, almost within sight of Buckingham Palace, *The Two Chairmen* perpetuates the memory of two of the ruffians who used to elbow their way through the crowds carrying the 'quality' in sedan chairs. George III bought Buckingham House just six years after *The Two Chairmen* opened, but it was little used as a palace until the 19th century, when it became the principal London home of the Sovereign. The Queen was not in residence when this photograph was taken: there is no Royal Standard flying over the Palace. (*Above and right*)

the Thames to St James's Park, stood the no longer seen Palace of Whitehall, the favourite Royal residence from 1530 to 1698. Originally known as York Place, it was the London residence of the Archbishops of York. In the reign of Henry VIII, Cardinal Wolsey lived here in far greater luxury than the King, so when Wolsey fell from grace in 1530, Henry was not slow to take over what he had long regarded as a very desirable property. As he annexed Hampton Court at the same time he was clearly the winner in an outsize game of real-life 'Monopoly'. The Banqueting House is, in fact, a Stuart replacement for an earlier Tudor hall and it must have dwarfed and outshone the comparatively modest Tudor buildings that surrounded it. It was designed by Inigo Jones, the son of a London clothworker who rose to become the first English architect in the modern sense of the word. He first came into contact with James I as a designer of scenery for court masques, an art form which he raised to such heights that Ben Jonson, the poet and dramatist, refused to collaborate with him on the grounds that his words were being overshadowed by the scenery.

The Banqueting House was completed in 1622 except for the magnificent Rubens ceiling which was commissioned by Charles I in 1629 when the painter-diplomat was on a visit to London. The painting took a further five years and the ceiling was not installed until 1635. It is ironical to realize that 14 years later Charles I must have walked beneath this very ceiling on his way to execution: the scaffold was erected outside the north front of the Banqueting House and a passage from it was knocked through the wall. Charles I had planned to rebuild the whole of the Palace of Whitehall in this new Italian style by Inigo Jones but, sadly for London, he did not have the opportunity. Inigo Jones himself died three years after the King's execution.

The remainder of Whitehall today is mainly Government offices of Victorian origin and permanence. Exceptions include the Admiralty (1725), the Horse Guards (1760) and parts of the Treasury building, designed by Sir John Soane, which are hidden behind its Victorian façade. Sir John Soane's own designs for improvements to the Houses of Parliament – done long before the 1834 fire – may be seen in his house, which is now a museum, in Lincoln's Inn Fields.

Off the north side of Whitehall is a house that attracts much public attention: No. 10 Downing Street. This, the official residence of Britain's Prime Ministers, is much larger than the modest front would suggest. The street is named after Sir George Downing who built the houses in it at the end of the 17th century. It was at No. 14, then part of the Colonial Office, that Wellington and Nelson are said to have met for the first and only time in their lives. The Duke recognized Nelson from his pictures, but Nelson was so impressed by this unknown man's conversation that he briefly left the room to inquire who he was.

The present Houses of Parliament are the result of an architectural competition organized a year after the Old Palace of Westminster had been destroyed. One rather restricting rule was that any design submitted must be in either the Gothic or Elizabethan style. Of the 97 entries submitted, 91 were Gothic, 6 Elizabethan. The winning entry was that of Charles Barry whose plans were accompanied by hundreds of drawings in exquisite detail of the proposed decoration and embellishments. It was not known until later that they were the work of Augustus Pugin, a dedicated Gothic revivalist, and it is to him as much as to Barry that the Houses of Parliament owe their appearance. The buildings were begun in 1840. The House of Lords was first used in 1847 and the House of Commons in 1852. The most famous feature is the clock tower popularly (though wrongly) known as 'Big Ben' which is strictly the nickname of the bell on which the hours are struck. The bell weighs $13\frac{1}{2}$ tons and was cast in Mears' foundry in Whitechapel in 1858. An earlier bell, cast at Norton near Stockton-on-Tees and nearly lost at sea on its journey to London, proved to be faulty. After only a few months in the tower it developed a crack and had to be broken up. 'Big Ben' was so named after Sir Benjamin Hall who was Commissioner of Works at the time.

Whitehall, running from Trafalgar Square to Parliament Square is certainly the grandest street in a city which is not noted for its civic planning, and it is one which millions hold in special reverence because of the Cenotaph, the non-denominational memorial to the dead of two World Wars. There was a time when few men passed it without removing their hats but, with changing fashions and dimming memories, this respectful custom lapsed many years ago. Now the Cenotaph emerges into prominence on the second Sunday in November when a vast Remembrance Day ceremony is held around it.

Whitehall may be the grandest street but the most regal is the Mall. This broad avenue, flanked by double rows of plane trees, leads from the forecourt of Buckingham Palace to Trafalgar

Square. Along its broad surface every Royal procession sets out on its triumphant way.

To the south of The Mall lies St James' Park, one of the many for which London is noted and envied. First laid out for Henry VIII as a deer park adjoining Whitehall Palace, it was re-modelled on more formal pleasure garden lines for Charles II and, finally, laid out once more very much in its present form for George IV by John Nash. From the delicate modern bridge which crosses the lake there is a most surprising view of London giving, towards Whitehall, the impression of an almost oriental city.

Standing on Westminster Bridge 170 years ago, William Wordsworth composed that often-quoted line: 'Earth has not anything to show more fair.' One wonders whether he would have written it today though he might well have re-tained that later line: 'A sight so touching in its majesty'

Without the armed services, the pageantry for which London is famous would barely exist. The Changing of the Guard which takes place every day outside Buckingham Palace and at Horse Guards in Whitehall; the Trooping of the Colour on the Queen's official birthday in June; Beating the Retreat on Horse Guards Parade; the Cenotaph Ceremony on Remembrance Sunday in November; Royal Salutes fired on birthdays and anniversaries and on the State Opening of Parliament; even the many open-air concerts in the London parks – all depend upon the musical proficiency and military precision of the Services, on their brilliant uniforms and well groomed horses, on their skill and discipline.

The Royal Salutes that loudly thump the air of Hyde Park make immensely exciting spectacles as well as audible reminders of state occasions,

and people are sometimes curious to know why those taking part should be known as the King's Troop of the Royal Horse Artillery when Britain has a Queen on the throne. Before the War the troop was known as the Riding Troop of the RHA; it was disbanded in 1939. On its revival after the War, King George VI asked that its name should be changed to the King's Troop, and Queen Elizabeth, on her accession in 1952, decided that the title should be retained in memory of her father. (*Left*)

Once every regiment had its own regimental band but economies in recent years have reduced their numbers very considerably. As a result the services of those that remain are very much in demand. All army bandsmen get their training at the Royal Military School of Music at Kneller Hall, Twickenham, once the home of the famous 17th century portrait painter, Sir Godfrey Kneller. (*Above*)

To those who are unfamiliar with or uninterested in the divisions within the Christian church, there is often some confusion between Westminster Abbey and Westminster Cathedral. To put it simply: Westminster Abbey is the premier church of the Church of England but not a cathedral: Westminster Cathedral is, of course, a cathedral but of the Roman Catholic Church. Westminster Cathedral is near Victoria Station on a site where the Westminster Bridewell prison stood until the late 19th century. It was bought by Cardinal Manning but it was his successor, Cardinal Vaughan, who commissioned John Bentley to prepare plans in the Italian or Byzantine style in 1894. His cathedral has been described as 'the nearest thing to Byzantium in London' but although Bentley wandered all over

Europe in search of inspiration, he is thought never to have reached what was then known as Constantinople. As the photograph shows the exterior is of red brick with stripes, arches and domes of stone. Inside, although there is still some brickwork exposed, most of it has been encased in glittering marble and mosaics.

It is a vast building 110m (360 feet) long, 47m (156 feet) wide and 36m (117 feet) to the roof of the nave. A major decorative element – the Stations of the Cross – was sculptured during World War I by Eric Gill who is perhaps best known for the figure of Ariel on the front of the BBC's Broadcasting House in Portland Place. The slender Campanile is 86m (284 feet) high and from its balcony there are extensive views all over London. (*Above*)

IN contrast to the opulent architecture of much of Whitehall, No. 10 Downing Street, the official home of Britain's Prime Ministers, presents a very modest façade to the world. But behind that famous and much photographed front door there is a much larger and more elegant house than the outside would suggest. It has, too, quite an extensive garden which is well hidden from the public gaze. The regular meetings of the Cabinet are usually held in the Cabinet Room on the ground floor. In front of its marble fireplace the long cabinet table is flanked by screens of Corinthian columns.

Many Prime Ministers, including Lord Melbourne and Sir Robert Peel and, in recent years, Mr Callaghan have used No. 10 mainly as an office, preferring to have their homes elsewhere. (*Left*)

ON the night of 16 October 1834, an architect named Charles Barry, who was travelling towards London on the coach from Brighton, observed a vivid red glow in the sky to the north.

An overheated flue pipe beneath the chamber used by the Lords had started a conflagration that spread to the whole of the Palace of Westminster. The only building of importance saved was the great hall built by William Rufus.

A few years later, the same Charles Barry, greatly assisted by Augustus Pugin who designed all the elaborate ornamentation and fitments, won the prize for the design of a new Palace of Westminster in competition with 96 other architects.

When all the restrictions under which Barry had to work are considered, it is remarkable that he was able to produce such a unified and satisfying overall grouping. The new Palace, in addition to incorporating the old Westminster Hall, provided debating chambers for both the Lords and the Commons and in addition some 500 separate rooms of varying sizes and uses. The foundation stone was laid in 1840 and though the palace was officially opened by Queen Victoria in 1852, the Victoria Tower was not

completed until 1860. As this photograph clearly demonstrates, the most satisfactory viewpoint is from the far side of the Thames in front of County Hall. From here the full majesty of the design can be appreciated – the balancing elements of the Victoria Tower and 'Big Ben', and the multitudinous pinnacles that stab the sky between.

Inside, it is the Lords' Chamber that best demonstrates the inventiveness of Pugin. Not an inch is unelaborated, not a niche unfilled, and the richness of his browns, golds and crimsons add majesty to this, the throne-room of Parliament.

Barry's Commons' debating chamber was destroyed by bombing during World War II and was hurriedly rebuilt. By October 1950 it was once again echoing to the lively exchanges of the Mother of Parliaments. (*Below*)

THE most conspicuous object in Trafalgar Square is, inevitably, Nelson's 45m (145 feet) column surmounted by a 5m (17 feet) statue of England's greatest naval hero. From this windswept height he keeps a weather eye on the Admiralty in Whitehall. The base of his column is guarded by four lions, sculptured by Sir Edwin Landseer and cast in bronze from the guns of the *Royal George* which sank with the loss of all hands off Spithead in 1782. But there is much more to Trafalgar Square than Nelson's column. There is, for instance, the excellent equestrian statue of Charles I gazing sadly down Whitehall towards the scene of his execution outside the Banqueting House in 1649. Around it on 30 January each year groups of Stuart supporters hold brief memorial services and lay wreaths to the King's memory.

Beyond the fountain in this picture is another equestrian statue – that of King George IV. It was originally on top of the Marble Arch which, until it was removed in 1851, was the gateway into the forecourt of Buckingham Palace.

Beyond the statue is the globe that surmounts the Coliseum theatre, the permanent home of the English National Opera Company. The church to the right is probably the most famous in London after St Paul's and Westminster Abbey. For over 50 years services have regularly been broadcast from St Martin-in-the-Fields and, on the first Sunday in October, the Costermongers' Harvest Festival service is held here – a joyful occasion with all the Pearly Kings and Queens of London attending in their finery. (*Left*)

EACH year on Remembrance Sunday in November the Cenotaph in Whitehall becomes, for two silent minutes, the heart of the Commonwealth when the Queen attends the short but moving ceremony to commemorate the dead of two world wars. The Cenotaph, designed by Sir Edwin Lutyens, was unveiled by King George V in 1920. (*Above*)

THERE is some magic ingredient in the evening
light that enriches London as darkness falls.
Buildings that stand almost unnoticed by day are
transformed into romantic silhouettes against the
peach and eggshell-blue of sunset skies. As the lights
come on along the Thames embankments, the
surface of the river breaks their reflection into
dancing fragments that scatter and re-form in the
wake of passing tugs. In some parts of London it is
possible to find an unfrequented courtyard or alley
that is still lit by a hissing Victorian gaslamp. It
would not be surprising to see Sherlock Holmes
alight from a hansom-cab by its hesitant glimmer.
Even the traffic lights that change so imperiously by
day assume a carnival gaiety against the velvet dusk.
As the commuters nudge their way homewards,
bumper to bumper, the flocks of starlings that have
spent their day prowling around the suburbs where
the pickings are rich, come wheeling in in their
thousands to roost on every available cornice, ledge
or crenellation, enjoying the warmth that the city
workers have generated and oblivious it seems, of
the neon signs that stab the dark. As London's
floodlights come on, stand on Waterloo Bridge and
see how St Paul's, the Tower of London, Somerset
House, the County Hall and the Houses of Parliament, isolated from their surroundings, achieve a
new and impressive dignity that is often denied them
by daylight with all its competing attractions.
London is at its most seductive as the sun goes down.
Constitution Hill (*right*) and Big Ben (*far right*)

WESTMINSTER Abbey is more than the Church of England's premier and noblest church – it is the repository of much of England's history since before the Norman Conquest.

Edward the Confessor re-founded it in 1055 as a Benedictine monastery, and the building was consecrated in 1065. Henry III rebuilt it in the 13th century to honour the memory of Edward who had been canonized in 1163. The master mason in charge of the building was almost certainly a Frenchman, Henry of Reims, and the French influence is seen in the system of chapels radiating from the ambulatory, the only example of this plan in England. In 1269, three years before Henry's death, the body of St Edward was transferred to the sumptuous new shrine that had been prepared to receive it. It is on the altar of St Edward's Chapel that the oil used in the Coronation ceremony is consecrated.

Since William the Conqueror nearly every king and queen of England has been crowned in the Abbey and most of those up to George II are buried there. One of the many magnificent tombs is that of Henry V in the form of a small chantry chapel. Henry VII's Chapel both externally and internally is a *tour de force* – an Abbey in miniature with nave, aisles and five radiating chapels beneath glorious fan-vaulting. In the north and south aisles of this chapel are the tombs of both Elizabeth I and Mary, Queen of Scots. In life they never met but in death they are nearby neighbours. (*Above*)

THE intended Palace at Whitehall, if it had been carried out, would have been the most truly magnificent and beautiful fabric of any of the kind in Europe.' This was Horace Walpole's opinion of the plans drawn up by Inigo Jones in the reign of James I for the rebuilding of the jumble of old palace buildings that lay between the Thames and what is now St James's Park. Only the Banqueting House in Whitehall was ever completed and, as can be seen from this photograph, Horace Walpole's verdict was no exaggeration. At the time of its building – 1622 – the London crowds, accustomed to the undisciplined styles of Elizabethan architecture, must have gasped in awe at this grand, beautifully proportioned, Italian-inspired masterpiece. In Stuart times the ground floor, now used for storage, was a private wine-grotto where the king could drink with his friends. The main apartment, used mainly for official functions and concerts, is 33.5m (110 feet) long and 17m (55 feet) broad and high – a double cube. The Rubens ceiling, installed in 1635, portrays the blessings of peace and prosperity which were conferred on the United Kingdom of England and Scotland by the wise rule of James I. (*Right*)

THE WEST END

HALF THE WORLD GOES SHOPPING IN London's 'West End'. Actors and actresses dream about having their names in lights in the 'West End'. People complain when out-of-town restaurants charge 'West End' prices. What exactly is the 'West End' and where is it found?

The Concise Oxford Dictionary is indeed concise about it. 'West End', it says, 'is the richer and more fashionable district of London'. All right in Victorian or Edwardian days, perhaps, when Mayfair, Marylebone and Belgravia housed the rich and fashion was their occupation. But in the more egalitarian days since two World Wars, is one part of London notably richer or more fashionable than another? The two don't necessarily go together any more. Today, 'West End' is more of a feeling and less of a fact. 'West End' is where the shops are – the best shops, of course. 'West End' is where the theatres are. 'West End' is where the pleasure is. And none of it is very far from Piccadilly Circus, London's traditional centre of gaiety.

Strictly speaking, Piccadilly Circus is more of a triangle than a circle. Its bewildering cross-hatch of traffic lanes is presided over by a cupid-like figure with bow and arrow popularly known as 'Eros'. Visitors to permissive London find it appropriate that Aphrodite's son should symbolize the city's pleasure-seeking centre, so it comes as a surprise to many to learn that 'Eros' is, in fact, part of a memorial fountain erected in 1892 by earnest Victorian admirers of Lord Shaftesbury, a noted philanthropist and social reformer, and that the figure was intended to be not the embodiment of physical love but the Angel of Christian Charity.

Westward from the Circus, Piccadilly stretches as far as Hyde Park Corner where a spacious, grassy but coldly impersonal round-about, threaded with subways and underpasses, has successfully uncorked one of London's most persistent bottlenecks. Between the two points there is architectural variation that few London

As the Tower of London symbolizes the City, and the Houses of Parliament Westminster, so the statue of Eros in Piccadilly Circus epitomizes London's West End – the London of smart shops, luxurious hotels, theatres, cinemas, nightclubs, discotheques and restaurants. (*Left*)

streets can outdo: St James' Church – Christopher Wren's own favourite – tucked away in its cool courtyard; Simpson's store, designed by Joseph Emberton back in 1935; Fortnum and Mason's grown-up grocer's shop with Mr Fortnum and Mr Mason personally striking the hours on a Disneyesque clock; Burlington House, home of the Royal Academy of Arts and many other learned societies, hiding some real charm behind a pretentious Victorian front; Burlington Arcade, a superior shopping precinct which, if the shops were not so eminently respectable, might be known as the 'Top Tourist Trap'; Hatchard's, the famous bookshop, with a façade that must be virtually unchanged since early Georgian times; the Ritz Hotel, a piece of Paris in Piccadilly designed by Mewes and Davis whose French inclination can be seen in many London buildings of the first half of this century.

Beyond the Ritz, on the south side of Piccadilly, all building ends. Here, suddenly, is verdant treescape – the Green Park undulating towards Constitution Hill and Buckingham Palace. In this park on 27 April 1749 'an exhibition of fireworks which in grandeur could not have been surpassed' was held to celebrate the Peace of Aix-la-Chapelle, and Handel's *Music for the Royal Fireworks* received its first performance. A contemporary print shows that what are now the gardens of Buckingham Palace were then part of the park.

From the desert island of Hyde Park Corner, round which the traffic tides constantly flow, the Duke of Wellington on his favourite charger, Copenhagen, gazes across Piccadilly towards the building which used to be known as No. 1 London – Apsley House, the Duke's home from 1817 onwards when he bought it from his brother after his victory at Waterloo. In 1947, the 7th Duke returned Apsley House to the nation and in 1952 it was opened as the Wellington Museum. Here can be seen many of the exquisite and fantastic gifts that a relieved Europe showered on its saviour after the defeat of Napoleon.

Some of the finest pictures in the museum – works by Goya, Velasquez, Correggio, Rubens, Brueghel the Elder, Jan Steen and Jan van der Heyden – were acquired when Joseph Napoleon's baggage train was captured during the Spanish campaign. Wellington – very correctly – offered

to return the pictures to Spain, but a grateful Spanish government pointed out that they had come into Wellington's possession 'by means that are as just as they are honourable' and that he was to keep them.

Park Lane runs north from Hyde Park Corner along the edge of the park. Today it is a dual carriageway of almost motorway proportions, but in Queen Anne's reign 'the lane leading from Piccadilly to Tyburn' was described as 'a desolate by-road'. At Tyburn, close to where the Marble Arch now stands, Londoners could, until 1783, watch public hangings. Dr. Johnson's biographer, James Boswell, was a regular spectator.

Some of London's most luxurious hotels look out across Park Lane to the inviting green acres of Hyde Park. After the execution of Charles I, it was auctioned off to the highest bidder, and realized £17,068 2s 8d. John Evelyn wrote in his diary for 11 April 1653: 'I went to take the aire in Hide Park, when every coach was made to pay a shilling and horse sixpence by the sordid fellow who had purchased it of the State'. At the Restoration of the Monarchy in 1660, all such sales were declared null and void. Hyde Park again became a Royal park (as it is today) and it was reopened to the public freely though the King retained the right to 'one-half of the pippins or red-streaks, either in apples or cider, as His Majesty may prefer'.

That famous landmark the Marble Arch effectively signals the western limit of London's West End. It was designed by John Nash and originally erected, at a cost of £80,000, at the entrance to Buckingham Palace. The equestrian statue of George IV, which now stands in Trafalgar Square, was intended to surmount it. The arch was moved to its present position in 1851.

Oxford Street, running east from Marble Arch for close on three km (two miles), is London's most concentrated shopping area, with stores that are household names side by side with newer, specialist shops anxious to get a foot in the door of this golden treasure house. Many of the stores have been in Oxford Street for well over a hundred years. Peter Robinson came down from Yorkshire to open his draper's shop in 1833. William Debenham, from Suffolk, was in business in nearby Wigmore Street even earlier. Marshall went into partnership with

Snelgrove in 1848. John Lewis left Peter Robinson's to set up on his own in 1864. And Dan H. Evans, a comparative newcomer from Llanelli in Wales, started up in Oxford Street in 1879. But it was in 1909 that Oxford Street first became the nation's – rather than fashionable London's – shopping mecca when Gordon Selfridge came over from Chicago to open his spectacular popular-price store. Not until 1930 did Marks and Spencer, surely the most successful merchandiser of all time, invade Oxford Street, though they had stores in the suburbs as early as 1903.

In Charles II's reign, 'He who then rambled to what is now [1850] the gayest and most crowded part of Regent Street, found himself in solitude, and was so fortunate sometimes as to have a shot at a woodcock.' Regent Street was designed by John Nash to be a triumphal way joining Carlton House, the Prince Regent's palatial Westminster home, with Marylebone Park in the northerly village of Marylebone, now Regent's Park. The building began in 1813 and as Nash had control of the design of all the buildings in the street, there was a continuity of design which made Regent Street one of the most admired architectural developments in Europe. The line of the street remains but all Nash's buildings are gone except at the north end of Portland Place where Park Crescent demonstrates the original Nash style.

These four streets – Piccadilly, Park Lane, Oxford Street and Regent Street – form the periphery of the square mile known as Mayfair. Though Mayfair is no longer exclusively the home of the wealthy (there is only one private house left in Berkeley Square) it retains an air of affluence, and this is especially noticeable in Bond Street, the High Street of Mayfair – 'high' referring only to quality and price.

By contrast – and much of London's charm stems from its many contrasts – the area east of Regent Street, on the far side of Golden Square (once a burial for the plague victims of 1665) is affluent in a different manner. Soho, as it is called, is one of the most cosmopolitan areas of any city in the world. Members of every race and nationality live and work here, making money mainly out of restaurants and other more dubious establishments. The restaurants are mostly first-class; the bookshops and strip clubs distinctly sleazy. On one side of Soho's main artery – Shaftesbury Avenue – theatres stand almost arm in arm. South of Shaftesbury Avenue, large, plush cinemas overlook Leicester Square. By and large, Soho makes a noisy, informal and fascinating appendage to London's West End'.

N ames change but the lights shine perennially in Shaftesbury Avenue, the central thoroughfare of London's eating and entertainment district of Soho. The name Soho derives from a hunting call, adopted by the Duke of Monmouth as his rallying cry at the battle of Sedgemoor in 1685, when Soho Square was being built where Monmouth House once stood. (*Right*)

Napoleon's remark about England being a nation of shopkeepers was not original. He misquoted it from Adam Smith who said nothing of the kind. But true or false, London is certainly the shopkeeper's shop-window, the apogee of merchandizing, the pinnacle of choice. And the fascinating thing about London shops is that they are not segregated – you don't find, for instance, a street that is all hat shops or a street that is all butchers. They are all gloriously mixed up, switching your attention from food to fashion to furniture and back again. The big stores – such as Harrods and Selfridges – are, of course, world famous. But equally famous are some of the small, specialist shops which have proliferated in recent years: shops that sell nothing but amber or slacks or door knobs. Noticeable, too, is the way street markets and little corner grocery shops still prosper close to the heart of London.

In Berwick Street, almost within sight of Piccadilly Circus, is the sort of street market you would expect to find in any country town – stalls lit by naked swinging bulbs, heaped high with every sort and variety of fruit and vegetable. As fascinating as the multi-coloured displays is the cockney banter of the stallholders. Salty epithets are served and returned across the street with the speed and precision of world-class tennis players. The prevailing mood is good humoured but the competition is fierce. (*Left*)

Hangover from the days when Jermyn Street was the village street of St James's is Paxton and Whitfield at No. 9. This is the shop that blind men can lead you to, guided by the pervading and beneficent odour of cheeses – hundreds of them, cheeses from England, Scotland, Ireland, France, Holland, Austria, Scandinavia, Italy and every other country where cheeses of quality are made. For, make no mistake: Paxton & Whitfield are masters of their trade, dealing only in cheeses that meet their exacting if old-fashioned standards. (*Right*)

Off the north side of Piccadilly, alongside Burlington House, a covered arcade of single storey shops leads through to Burlington Gardens. This is the Burlington Arcade, the most exclusive shopping precinct in London. During shopping hours (it closes after dark) it is full from end to end with tourists, a United Nations of shoppers, magnetized by the opulent displays of cashmeres and cameras, silver, shirts, pewter, ivory, tweeds, linen, leather – 'infinite riches in a little room'. The arcade was built as a bazaar by Lord George Cavendish, afterwards Earl of Burlington, in 1819. It was unworthily refronted in 1911. (*Left*)

BERKELEY Square, the Victorians used to say, was full of plane trees and hansom cabs. The magnificent trees are still there, only a few years younger than the square itself which was laid out in 1740. The hansom cabs have given way to handsome cars, mostly from showrooms on the east side of the square where the enormous pile of Berkeley Square House has swallowed up No. 17 Bruton Street, the house where the Queen was born in 1926. The square still provides a calm, pleasant oasis amid the swirling traffic of the West End. (*Above left*)

FRANKLIN Delano Roosevelt, three times president of the United States, has a special place in the affections of the British because of the moral and material support he gave to Britain at the time she stood alone against the Nazis. Thousands contributed to this fine memorial to him in Grosvenor Square, sculptured by Sir William Reid Dick. The American Embassy is visible behind the trees on the west side of the square. (*Left*)

TEA (the meal, not the drink) which used to be such a traditional event in the days when aunts took nephews and nieces to the pantomime, is now becoming harder to find in London. There is certainly the Ceylon Tea Centre and Fortnum's, but to the traditionalist, the Ritz Hotel is the dowager of them all. Here, in the Palm Court, in all its Rococo splendour, it is still possible to order thin cucumber sandwiches and be served by an attentive waiter. (*Above*)

JOHN Nash's Regent Street disappeared for ever in the 1920s, but the Quadrant – the curve that diverts the street into Piccadilly Circus – was part of his plan to give it what a visiting German admirer called its 'peculiar beauty'. This famous street is lined with some of London's finest shops – less pricey than Bond Street, less strident than Oxford Street. (*Left*)

To MANY VISITORS AND, INDEED, TO MANY Londoners, the district north of Oxford Street – Bloomsbury and Marylebone – is *terra incognita*. A visitor may cross it on his way to Euston Station, or a Londoner may penetrate it minimally on his apprehensive way to keep an appointment with a specialist in Harley Street but, by and large, the area is left to its own devices, to the satisfaction of its many residents. The Euston Road roars across it from west to east but on either side there is relative calm. Not that the area is without tourist attractions. Within its bounds are Regent's Park, the Zoo, Lord's Cricket Ground, Madame Tussaud's and the Planetarium, the Courtauld Institute Galleries, the Jewish Museum, the Wallace Collection, the Wellcome Medical Museum, the Post Office Tower and – crown jewel of them all – the British Museum. What has given the area its character is the fact that it was a guinea-pig for the ideas of the early town planners – something the rest of growing London didn't benefit from – and the planning took place in a period during which English architecture experienced its finest flowering – the 18th century.

Bloomsbury, bounded by Euston Road, Gray's Inn Road, High Holborn and New Oxford Street, and Tottenham Court Road, was earlier known as Lomesbury. It was merely a village on the outskirts of London where the King's horses were stabled and his hunting hawks were kept. Writing (in the 19th century) of the neighbourhood in the year 1685, Lord Macaulay, in his *History of England*, says: 'A little way north from Holborn and on the verge of pastures and cornfields, rose two celebrated palaces, each with an ample garden. One of them, then called Southampton House and, subsequently, Bedford House, was removed early in the present century to make room for a new city which now covers with its squares, streets and churches a vast area renowned in the seventeenth century for peaches and snipes. The other, known as Montagu House, celebrated for its furniture and frescoes, was, a few months after the death of Charles II, burned to the ground and was succeeded by a more magnificent Montagu House which, having long been the repository for such various and precious treasures of art, science and learning as were scarce ever before assembled under a single roof, has

given place to an edifice more magnificent still.'

Macaulay's 'new city' was, of course, Bloomsbury and 'the edifice more magnificent still' the newly built British Museum. The architectural style of Bloomsbury blossoms fully in Bedford Square, developed in 1775 by the Duke of Bedford who owned most of the land in the district. The square was designed as an entity by Thomas Leverton, later an unsuccessful contestant for the rebuilding of Regent Street. As is sometimes the way with architects, he reserved the best of the houses – No. 1 Bedford Square – for his own occupation. One of his neighbours was Thomas Wakeley who founded the still successful medical journal, *The Lancet*. Another was Lord Eldon, the then Lord Chancellor who grew – and ripened – grapes in his garden, regardless of the fact that his wife was an ardent teetotaller.

Bedford Square is happily so little altered that its present appearance gives a good idea of what much of Bloomsbury must have looked like in its heyday. Signs of the area's architectural good manners can also be seen in Bloomsbury Square, Gordon Square, Tavistock Square and Bedford Row, but much that gave Bloomsbury its town-planned appearance has been pulled down, and when juggernauts like the Senate House of London University, with its 64 m (210 ft) tower, are dropped into the heart of a Georgian town, balance is inevitably lost.

The British Museum is vast. People have been known to spend their lives there; others to 'do' it in a couple of hours. The fact is you are striding the corridors of a solid, three dimensional Encyclopaedia Britannica and you have to be selective. But what a boon it must be to the 40,000 students of London University. University College – the heart of the University – was founded in 1826 to provide 'literary and scientific education at a moderate expense'. The architect of the college, which is in Gower Street, was William Wilkins who also designed the National Gallery. It was opened in 1828, just 18 months after the laying of the foundation stone.

Just as Bloomsbury developed around Bedford Square, so Marylebone's growth may be said to have stemmed from Cavendish Square. The project was begun in 1715 when Lady Henrietta Harley, daughter of the Duke of Newcastle, inherited her father's Marylebone estate.

Her husband, Lord Harley (later to become 2nd Earl of Oxford and Mortimer) was a wealthy man and able to enlist the help of the very best architects and builders. For his architect he chose James Gibbs who later designed the church of St Martin-in-the-Fields. Building began in 1717 but three years later the South Sea Bubble, the notorious financial scandal which involved everyone from the King down, hit Lord Harley very severely and the development of Cavendish Square came almost to a halt. A view of the square, dated 1754, shows it far from complete with the north side still open to the fields as far as Hampstead. Twenty years earlier an architectural critic had written: 'I am morally assured that more people are displeased at seeing this square lie in its present neglected condition than are entertained with what was meant for elegance or ornament in it.' As late as 1761 there were still gaps in the north side where Lord Chandos had planned to build 'a palatial residence'. He, poor man, had died of a broken

The old Duke would feel much more at home in Woburn Walk, a short way up the road towards Euston station. Here the Georgian shop fronts with elegant, slim wrought iron balustrades are straight out of the 18th century. They look out on to a paved pedestrian walk full of tubs of flowers. These glimpses of Bloomsbury's Georgian past serve to emphasize what a handsome area it must have been and – in parts – still is. (*Right*)

Although his statue still presides over Russell Square, Francis, fifth Duke of Bedford, who died in 1805, would hardly recognize it today. Five years before his death he had commissioned Humphrey Repton to lay out a square worthy of the family name, Russell.

A few of the original houses, now somewhat altered, survive on the west side. Vast hotels, with a view over the square to the Senate House of London University, have taken over the east side, and Repton's gardens have been wholly changed with cascading fountains and lighting among the trees after dark. (*Below*)

heart after seeing his son and heir die in church while being baptized. His plans survive – and they may be seen in the British Museum.

All the streets which were subsequently developed around Cavendish Square are named after members of Lord Harley's family or the families into which he and his daughter married: Portland, Henrietta, Harley, Wigmore, Wimpole, Mortimer, Holles, Vere, Welbeck and Bentinck. An even stronger influence on the development of Marylebone was that of the Prince Regent (later George IV) and his favourite architect, John Nash. The Prince became Nash's patron and encouraged him to visualize the area between Oxford Street and Marylebone Park as a landscaped city matching the elegance of Venice with the scale of Versailles. Part of the Prince's dream was to link Carlton House, his home in the Mall with a new palace that John Nash would build for him in Regent's Park. The link would be a triumphal way – the finest street in Europe. John Nash was allowed to build Regent Street but not on the magnificent scale the Prince Regent visualized. The palace never materialized: the Prince lost interest in it when he became George IV on the death of his father. As recompense, John Nash was asked to convert Buckingham House into Buckingham Palace.

Nash, faced with problems and opposition, pressed on with the Regent's Park project, transforming the featureless heath of Marylebone into the handsome park we know today, studding its surroundings with opulent terraces and villas that quickly became, if not the wonder, at least the admiration of Europe. We admire Nash's vision and style today, but at the time he was not without his critics. Some feared that under the Prince's influence Nash might dot Regent's Park with a series of Brighton Pavilions. The *Quarterly Review* for June 1826 commented in verse:

> Augustus at Rome was for building renowned,
> And of marble he left what of brick he had found;
> But is not our Nash, too, a very great master?
> He finds us all brick and he leaves us all plaster.

Of the 56 villas Nash planned for the park, few were ever completed. Winfield House, built by the Woolworth heiress Barbara Hutton in 1937, is on the site of one of them. It is now the London home of the United States ambassador. Bedford College, a college of London University, has grown out of South Villa and is almost surrounded by the lake.

A newcomer to Regent's Park, reflecting the multiracial face that London is developing, is the Mosque, recently built in the grounds of the Islamic Cultural Centre. Where it stands was once the site of Albany Cottage, the home of Thomas Raikes, the profligate crony of Beau Brummell and the Prince Regent. One wonders if Mohammed approves ❧

THE Wallace Collection is generally thought to have been the most valuable gift that any nation has ever received from a private individual. It is without question one of the greatest art collections in the world. It is housed in what is externally a fairly unremarkable building – Hertford House – dating mainly from 1872. Internally it reveals the continuous good taste of the Marquesses of Hertford and, finally of the fourth Marquess's illegitimate son, Sir Richard Wallace, whose widow, knowing his wishes in the matter, gave the house and collection to the nation. It was opened to the public in 1900 and, because it is rather off the beaten tourist track – in Manchester Square (roughly behind Selfridges) –

it is possible to view the collection in unhurried comfort at almost any time of the day.

The Hertfords were either lucky or far-sighted in that their taste was predominantly French and they were buying at a time when the French Revolution and its aftermath had greatly lowered the demand for French art. In addition to the superlative French paintings and furniture of the 18th century, there are fine examples of Dutch, Flemish, Spanish and Italian art – Franz Hals' *Laughing Cavalier* and Rubens' *Rainbow Landscape* to name but two of the widely known masterpieces. There is, too, a unique collection of armour, majolica ware, church ornaments, porcelain, bronzes and clocks. (*Left*)

MANY people are discouraged from visiting the British Museum by the *embarras de choix* that confronts them. Shall they make for the Elgin Marbles? The Assyrian and Babylonian collections? The Egyptian Rooms with the historic Rosetta Stone (which enabled the hieroglyphics on the tombs and antiquities to be deciphered)? The beautifully displayed Roman and Western Asiatic antiquities? The 7th century Sutton Hoo burial ship? The Lindisfarne Gospels? Two surviving copies of Magna Carta? Or the fabulous Mildenhall Treasure turned up by a Suffolk farmer's plough in 1942? As at all banquets it is necessary to be abstemious or suffer the penalty of indigestion.

The British Museum's treasures have been accumulating steadily since 1753 when Sir Hans Sloane, the physician, bequeathed his valuable collection of books and manuscripts to the nation for a payment of £20,000 to his executors – an irresistible bargain. A lottery raised £100,000, and the British Museum was established in Montagu House, to be replaced a hundred years later by the present formidable building. (*Above*)

ALTHOUGH midsummer nights are unpredictable in London, the Open-Air Theatre in Regents Park, founded in 1933, has managed to survive and even prosper. It specializes in Shakespeare's more light-hearted plays and there is alternative covered accommodation should the weather fail to live up to the arcadian surroundings. (*Above*)

LONDON'S Moslem population has risen greatly in the past 30 years, and although the Moslem, provided he turns towards Mecca, can perform his act of worship wherever he happens to be, he is required to attend a mosque on Fridays to recite prayers in public and to hear a sermon. This mosque, adjacent to the Islamic Cultural Centre in Regent's Park, has been built to meet the needs of London's many followers of Mohammed. (*Below*)

DO not be misled by this very modern aviary, designed by Lord Snowdon: the London Zoo has been in Regent's Park since 1828, two years after the founding of the Zoological Society of London by Sir Stamford Raffles (of Singapore fame) 'for the advancement of zoology, and the introduction and exhibition of subjects of the animal kingdom, alive or in a state of preservation'. Since then literally millions of people have visited the Zoo or its country branch at Whipsnade, north of London. (*Right*)

ONE of the many 'narrow-boat' barges on Regent's Canal, which flows through Regent's Park, connecting the Grand Union Canal with the Thames at Limehouse. Many like this one are used as houseboats, moored in the area of wharf and canal known as Little Venice. (*Previous pages*)

THE Prince Regent's ambitious plans in collaboration with his favourite architect, John Nash, to build a triumphal route from Carlton House to Regent's Park, were never fully consummated. But indications of what might have been achieved are to be seen in Park Crescent, just south of the park, at the top of Portland Place. The plainness of the upper storeys is cleverly contradicted by the ground floor colonnades of twin Ionic columns. Portland Place itself has suffered architectural vandalism over the years, but Park Crescent is a worthy prelude to the park. (*Below*)

THE supreme example of Victorian self-confidence and conviction that the railway age would last for ever is St Pancras, the cathedral of all railway termini, and the subject of continuing architectural controversy. The saint himself – St Pancras – is rarely discussed but he was a young Phrygian nobleman who suffered martyrdom at Rome under the Emperor Diocletian for his adherence to the Christian faith. Because he was only 14 when he died he is generally known as the patron saint of children.

The railway station named after him was built between 1868 and 1874 by Sir George Gilbert Scott. The front on to Euston Road was the 600-room Midland Grand Hotel adapted from Sir George's rejected plan for a new Foreign Office. As the railway dream faded the hotel reverted to the purpose of the original design – offices. (*Right*)

AN OLD HINDU LEGEND TELLS HOW THREE men, confronted with an elephant in a darkened room, attempt to describe it. One, touching the trunk, says it must be like a water-pipe. The second, encountering its ear, finds it to be like a fan. The third, feeling its leg, says it must resemble a pillar of the temple. None is able to relate the part he encounters to the whole.

Describing the Royal Borough of Kensington and Chelsea poses a similar problem. How typical of Kensington as a whole are the grassy acres of Kensington Gardens? Or the noise and bustle of the bus-cluttered High Street? Or the conspicuous elegance of Montpelier Square? Or the faded gentility of Notting Hill? Kensington's common denominator is elusive. It shares with so much of the rest of the city the miscellaneousness that makes London such an endearing, fascinating, elephantine place.

Kensington and Chelsea add up to the smallest of the inner London boroughs, though it is clearly one of the wealthier and more fashionable, and the Greater London Council blue plaques, marking the former homes of the famous, are thick on the walls.

Up to the middle of the 19th century, Kensington was little more than an overgrown village in the county of Middlesex. In 1899 it became a London borough and the council presented an address to Queen Victoria asking her to confer some special distinction on the newly created borough to perpetuate the memory of her birth in Kensington Palace. At that time Kensington Palace was technically within the London boundary, but an adjustment was hastily made to transfer it from Westminster to Kensington. Before Kensington's request could be granted, the Queen had died, but her wishes in the matter were well known and King Edward VII conferred the title 'Royal' on the borough in 1901, making it England's third royal borough – the other two being Kingston-upon-Thames and Windsor. The honour brought no special privileges with it though one offender when arrested by the police insisted that as a resident of a Royal borough he was entitled to be taken to the police station in a cab – a luxury that the police made certain was not shared by any future offenders.

Though officially recognized in 1901, Kensington's ascent to royal status had been going on for many years. In 1689, William III, whose asthma was exacerbated by the fogs and fumes of Whitehall, bought Nottingham House, one of the finest properties in the village, for £18,000. Sir Christopher Wren was given the task of converting it into Kensington Palace, which he did under the watchful and often critical eye of Queen Mary who, during the alterations, stayed at Holland House, much of which is still to be seen in Holland Park.

Five years after the royal couple had moved into Kensington Palace, Queen Mary died of smallpox and, eight years later, William III fell from his horse while riding at Hampton Court, developed pneumonia and died at the early age of 51, to be succeeded by his sister-in-law Anne. Queen Anne, with the aid of 100 gardeners, had the grounds laid out in a less formal, more English style and commissioned Nicholas Hawksmoor (though some say it was Wren) to build the orangery, a delightful feature of the gardens. Twelve years later, Queen Anne was dead and George I hastened from Hanover to claim the throne. He made extensive alterations to the palace and once again the gardens were redesigned more to the Hanoverian taste. At this time they covered more than 120 hectares (300 acres) of what is today Kensington Gardens including the Round Pond. George II allowed selected members of Society to use the gardens but, at the beginning of the 19th century, George III opened the gardens to 'respectably dressed' members of the public and they have remained open ever since. Today Princess Margaret, Countess of Snowdon, occupies part of the palace.

Kensington Palace has an astonishingly rural outlook towards the Long Water, as the upper part of the Serpentine is called. The horse ride known as Rotten Row began life as an 'infamously bad' coach road from Kensington Palace to Whitehall – the *route du roi*. Englishmen always have managed to massacre the French language!

The southern fringe of Kensington Gardens, curtained with blossom and carpeted with daffodils in the spring, borders the busy part of the Kensington Road known as Kensington Gore which separates the Albert Memorial from the Albert Hall – a part of London dedicated to the memory of Queen Victoria's much mourned husband, Albert, the Prince Consort who died in 1861. The site of the Albert Memorial is a few hundred yards west of the scene of the Great Exhibition of 1851 in which Albert had played such an outstanding part. The Albert Hall, which had a shaky start (there was a financial panic in 1866) was ultimately paid for by the sale of 999-year leases of seats and boxes. It was opened by Queen Victoria on 29 March 1871 and is probably best known today as the home of the BBC's annual season of promenade concerts.

THE former separate boroughs of Kensington and Chelsea are now administratively combined, Kensington retaining its 'Royal' prefix and Chelsea inevitably sharing the glory. Both have always been fashionable residential areas, and the enlarged borough is very densely populated.

In the two decades between 1860 and 1880 the population of Kensington and Chelsea more than doubled and there was a tremendous boom in housing, so there are many examples of the domestic architecture of that period still to be seen. The main change has been that the large houses of the wealthy middle-class are now divided into flats, and the one-time workmen's terraced cottages and mews coach-houses have become much sought-after 'bijou residences'. (*Left and right*)

Just behind the Albert Hall, the Royal Horticultural Society had a 9 hectare (22 acre) garden until 1882. Their present gardens are at Wisley in Surrey, but they continue to hold their main annual flower show in the Borough – in the grounds of the Royal Hospital, Chelsea. This handsome range of buildings, designed by Wren, was commissioned by Charles II prompted (an improbable legend asserts) by Nell Gwyn whose sympathy for destitute soldiers was likely to be keener than that of her king's. James II had come and gone and William and Mary were on the throne before the hospital was occupied in 1692. The scarlet dress uniform of the pensioners, heavy with medals and years, is a familiar sight throughout London. The army's own splendid new museum is a mere hand-grenade's throw from the hospital.

King's Road, running west from Sloane Square, was originally a private track crossing the orchards and market gardens of Chelsea and Fulham and reserved for the convenience of Charles II on his amorous outings to Sandford Manor House, where Nell Gwyn lived, and to Hampton Court, where several other of his mistresses were likely to be found. Today it is one of the most cosmopolitan streets in London and a showplace for all that is new, eccentric and non-conformist.

Where Beaufort Street leads down from King's Road to Battersea Bridge was the site of Beaufort House, the Chelsea riverside home of Sir Thomas More – the 'Man for All Seasons'. His 16th century house, demolished in 1740, was described by More's friend Erasmus as 'neither mean nor subject to envy, yet magnificent and commodious enough'. It was More's resistance to Henry VIII's claim that the King and not the Pope was head of the Church that cost Sir Thomas his head. His body probably lies buried in the Chapel of St Peter in the Tower of London, but there is a memorial to him in Chelsea Old Church where he used to worship. The More Chapel was a gift from Sir Thomas in his own lifetime.

A most prominent feature of Kensington is its museums – the Victoria and Albert, the Science Museum, the Natural History Museum and the Geological Museum. Their combined collections are so vast and so comprehensive that it would be invidious to compare them. Their solid Victorian exteriors give no hint of the excitement and stimulation within.

As a shopping centre Kensington is certainly the equal in quality, if not in quantity, to the West End. It is the home of probably the most famous store in the world – Harrods. Dating from 1861 when Charles Harrod, son of an East Anglian miller, opened his grocer's shop at No. 8 Middle Queen Buildings, Brompton Road,

Harrod's reputation was built on the excellence of the goods he sold and the high standard of personal attention he gave to his customers. Even today, though the store is now part of the House of Fraser empire, there is a felicity about shopping at Harrods that goes a long way towards justifying their generally higher prices. Further west in Kensington High Street, John Barker opened his store in 1870 and it is still going strong, having absorbed the rival Pontings store in 1906. Woollands and Derry and Toms have faded from the commercial scene but in Sloane Square, Peter Jones, a branch of the John Lewis Partnership, is keeping very much in step with the times. Its up-to-the-minute-looking building is in fact more than forty years old.

Another building which deserves a visit is the Commonwealth Institute – a dull sounding name for an exciting place. In fact, the same might be said of Kensington itself

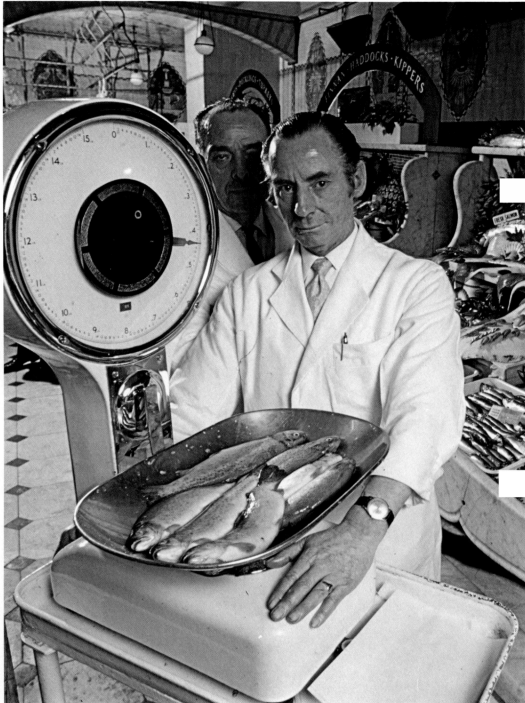

For nearly 300 years the Chelsea Pensioners have been residents of Chelsea, and recognized all over London by the scarlet (in summer) and blue (in winter) uniforms which they have inherited from those worn by the Duke of Marlborough's troops in the 18th century. The grounds of their home – the Royal Hospital – are generally open but for one week in the year (in May) they are the scene of one of the most colourful events of the London season: the Royal Horticultural Society's Chelsea Flower Show. (*Left*)

Harrods may be technically in Westminster but it is, at heart, part of that more westerly shopping area that takes in Sloane Square and Kensington High Street. It is said to be the largest departmental store in Europe, and who would dispute it as one glides across acres of deep-pile carpeting and escalates silently from fish to furs. All under one roof you can bank or buy a house or select a Shetland pony for your daughter. You may not know what you need but Harrods will undoubtedly have it. (*Above*)

BETWEEN them Hyde Park and Kensington Gardens make up 250 hectares (616 acres) of precious land right in the heart of London – land which no one since Cromwell has ever tried to dispose of. Kings and Queens from time to time annexed portions of Kensington Gardens for their private enjoyment, but for nearly 200 years Londoners have had free access to both parks. Queen Caroline, wife of George II, ordered the damming of the Westbourne stream to form the Serpentine – the distinctive elongated stretch of water that is shared between the two parks. Above the Serpentine Bridge it is known as the Long Water. From it the Round Pond in Kensington Gardens is fed. Fishing is not permitted in the Long Water, and before skating is allowed the ice must be at least five inches thick. (*Above*)

ANYONE may ride in Rotten Row – the anglicized 'route du roi' – but, as the notice says 'Galloping is not allowed'. By utilizing every yard of horse ride in the Park and then crossing over Hyde Park Corner to the horse tracks in Constitution Hill and the Mall, it is possible to trot for about six km (nearly four miles) right in the heart of London without covering the same ground twice. (*Right*)

IN former times, Hyde Park stretched right up to where Kensington Palace stands. When William III made it his home he 'borrowed' 10 hectares (26 acres) of the park for his front garden. Later Queen Anne enlarged the gardens and, by the reign of George II the palace gardens had absorbed the whole of Kensington Gardens as they are today. The famous Round Pond, which is more correctly a rectangle with rounded corners, is London's model yacht Mecca. The statue of Queen Victoria in front of the palace was sculptured by the Queen's talented daughter, Princess Louise, later Marchioness of Lorne. Adjoining the palace is an orangery designed either by Wren or Hawksmoor and built in 1704. The iron gates leading into Kensington Gardens are left-overs from the Great Exhibition of 1851. (*Far right*)

ANY similarity between the Albert Memorial and St Pancras station (see page 49) is not coincidental: Sir George Gilbert Scott was the architect of both. The Albert Memorial he regarded as his 'most prominent work'. Its prominence is undeniable – a 53m (175 feet) pinnacle of Victorian exuberance and genuine respect for Prince Albert, contributed to by the outstanding sculptors of the day. The memorial was erected out of public subscriptions and with the surplus a start was made on the Albert Hall on the other side of Kensington Gore. It is a vast amphitheatre, seating 8,000 people in three tiers of boxes and a balcony. Its acoustic properties were something of a joke for many years (the Albert Hall echo was very persistent) but modern technology seems to have overcome the problem satisfactorily. (*Left*)

UNTIL it was virtually destroyed in the *Blitz*, Holland House (behind the Commonwealth Institute in Kensington High Street) was the last country house estate in the heart of London. Its extensive grounds are now one of the Greater London Council's many parks and part of the ruined house has been rebuilt as a very popular Youth Hostel. Another part of the house has been adapted to provide a backdrop for the Court Theatre which presents open-air plays, operas and recitals. The sun-filled Orangery with its classical bronze figures is a delightful feature of the gardens. (*Below*)

THE Notting Hill district of Kensington contrasts fiercely with the rather staid, middle-class area south of Holland Park Avenue. Here there has been a tremendous influx of Commonwealth immigrants, bringing to the rather drab district much of the lively, colourful and extroverted behaviour of the Caribbean. Every summer the local immigrant organizations promote a street carnival spread over two days which is one of the noisiest, most colourful and most spontaneous events in London. Unhappily, in recent years, the carnival has too often ended on a note of violence started, it is generally thought, by some external element out to provoke the police. (*Above*)

PORTOBELLO Road, just north of Notting Hill Gate underground station, is synonymous with the street market that takes place here every week-day. Saturday is the day for antique bargain hunters when the most unlikely and bizarre objects are bought and sold, swapped and haggled over. Visiting antique dealers are usually on the prowl, so the chance of picking up a genuine bargain is fairly remote, and most of the stallholders are pretty knowledgeable too. The better quality goods are more likely to be found in Collectors' Corner and the Portobello Arcade – stalls within buildings rather than at the roadside. The market is the happy hunting ground for Victoriana, though when Queen Victoria came to the throne what is now the Portobello Road was part of Portobello Farm, named after the city that was captured by Admiral Vernon in the War of the Austrian Succession. (*Left*)

THE THAMES

THE THAMES MAY NOT RATE A PLACE IN THE list of the world's greatest rivers but it is often one of England's loveliest, and for many centuries, its busiest.

To many people today the Thames seems to be sadly under-used. The London docks are in decline, trade having moved towards the estuary, to Tilbury and beyond. The wide water highway still cuts through the centre of the City but a passing boat is now something to stop and stare at. The ships that are moored in central London are now mostly museums. However, all is far from lost. Just over a century ago the Thames was an open sewer, fish were driven from its putrid waters, cholera and typhoid were rampant. Today its waters are relatively pure. Nearly 100 different species of fish have returned to the river. It is firmly expected that salmon will once again thrive in it as they did in the 19th century when more than 400 fishermen between Westminster and Deptford made a living from the Thames. Then, the noblemen who occupied the great houses along what is now the Strand, regularly swam for pleasure in the river, and Lord Byron refers in a letter to the occasion on which he swam the five km (three miles) from Lambeth to London Bridge.

In the 19th century, the great growth of London's population and its spreading industrialization became too much for the Thames: sewage and pollution swamped it, and drastic action had to be taken. A huge sewage system for London was incorporated in the Victoria Embankment, completed in 1865 and involving the reclamation of 15 hectares (37 acres) from the river. Today London's sewage system depends on Thames water to maintain its flow, and almost half of London's fresh water requirements – about 400 million gallons a day – are met from the Thames. Above Westminster the use of the river for water sports is growing yearly and the upper reaches have never been more popular since Jerome K. Jerome wrote his perennial classic, *Three Men in a Boat*.

So much of the Thames in London has been embanked or industrially developed that it is cheering to come across a stretch that must look much as it has done for the past 200 years – a stretch of the north bank below Kew Bridge known as Strand-on-the-Green. Here, a collection of smallish houses of mixed styles and periods face boldly on to the river, separated from what would seem to be inevitable flooding by nothing more defensive than a narrow, willow-bordered footpath. (*Above*)

TEN miles further up the river, Hampton Court spreads itself in brick-red splendour, high above any possible flooding and guarded by twelve majestic wrought-iron screens or gates. These delicate, tough and charming masterpieces were certainly designed – and probably made – by a Frenchman named Jean Tijou, who also did much of the ironwork for St Paul's. The screens were ordered by William III in 1694 and the WM (William and Mary) monogram can be seen over the gates. They have occupied different positions in the grounds at different times

and even spent 35 years in the South Kensington Museum, from where they were returned in 1902. Through the tracery of the gates can be seen the east front of the Fountain Court, part of Sir Christopher Wren's extensive addition to the palace. (*Left*)

From its source in the Cotswold Hills, the Thames alternately cascades and meanders for more than 320 km (200 miles) towards the North Sea. About one quarter of the journey is spent in London, broad between banks, idling past the manifold activities of man and nature. So the 65 km (49 miles) between Hampton Court (where the Thames enters Greater London) and Crayford Ness (where it leaves it behind) are full of visual interest and, in the immortal (if unaspirated) words of John Burns, 'liquid 'istory'.

The history begins right away at Hampton Court, for here is the magnificent Tudor palace, built by Cardinal Wolsey, designed to accommodate 400 guests and 500 servants. On his fall from royal favour, Wolsey forfeited everything to Henry VIII who enlarged it still further. Later additions, designed by Wren, were made by William III who found, in the fresh, up-river air, relief from his chronic asthma brought on by the sulphurous fumes of London.

From here to Kingston the Thames is still an up-country river, alive in summer with small craft, bordered with houseboats that rock gently to the swell of Oxford-bound launches. Kingston-upon-Thames (to give it its full title) is a royal borough, the crowning place of Saxon kings – and the town has a coronation stone to prove it. Until 1730, Kingston Bridge was the first road crossing above London Bridge.

At Teddington (Tide-ending-town) the river dives over its last down-stream weir – an average flow of 1,000 million gallons a day – and the tidal river begins, its twice daily rise and fall providing a gentle reminder that the cruel sea is now not far away.

Past Strawberry Hill and Twickenham, the river flows through the elegant arches of Richmond's humpback bridge, the oldest still spanning the river in London. It was built in 1774 but widened and somewhat de-humped in 1937.

Adjoining Richmond's Old Deer Park (once part of Richmond Palace where Elizabeth I died in 1603) Kew Gardens welcome anyone who cares to take the poet's advice to 'Go down to Kew in lilac time', and admission is still only one penny.

By Chiswick Bridge there are acres of sports grounds followed, appropriately, by the famous Mortlake brewery which dominates the finish of one of the thirstiest events in the sporting calendar: the Oxford and Cambridge boat race. From here to Putney Bridge, where the race begins, the winding 6·8 km (4¼ miles) of river is lined with landmarks that are familiar to those who follow this annual event: Barnes Bridge, Harrods Repository, Chiswick Eyot, Hammersmith Bridge, Fulham Football Ground, the Mile Post and Putney Bridge itself.

Up to 1884, when the present bridge was built, Putney Bridge was a constant object of criticism and complaint, forcing one visitor to write: 'The decayed and apparently dangerous state of Putney Bridge, an ugly, black structure of timber with no feature to recommend it, cannot fail to disgust the observer.'

Beyond the Hurlingham Club, where polo was played until the last war, both banks of the Thames have become thickly industrialized but, hidden away near the chimneys of Lots Road on the north bank, it is said to be possible to find the remains of Sandford Manor House, where Nell Gwyn lived.

At Chelsea, the elegant terrace houses of Cheyne Walk face the river. Around here the Greater London Council's blue plaques that mark the former homes of the famous are numerous: 'Mark Twain', Leigh Hunt, Oscar Wilde, Captain Scott, Mrs Gaskell, the Brunels, George Eliot and Thomas Carlyle among them.

The Thames is now approaching the heart of London and once through Lambeth Bridge the full panorama of the city comes into view, from the dominating Victoria Tower of the House of Lords, down river to St Paul's, now dwarfed by the hectic, vertical architecture that has fractured the old city skyline, round past the concrete complex of the South Bank, past County Hall, the headquarters of the Greater London Council. The new, high block of St Thomas's Hospital still gives its patients one of the finest views in London and a front row seat for Big Ben's hourly concerts. The great sweep ends at one of London's least appreciated treasures: Lambeth Palace, the medieval home of the Archbishop of Canterbury.

This is the Thames that did duty as the main street of London for 1,000 years. This was the scene of constant processions and pageantry, but in recent years, apart from the funeral of Sir Winston Churchill and the Queen's Silver Jubilee River Pageant, the Thames has not taken much part in the nation's ceremonial. Ever since the middle of the 17th century, water processions dwindled as road transport improved. Yet, as late as 1820, when George IV came to the throne, there were still 3,000 wherries plying for hire on the Thames, while the highroad alternative – the Hackney carriage – numbered only 1,200 throughout the whole of London. Back in the 16th century there were said to be 40,000 water-

men on the river between Windsor and Gravesend.

From the Tower to Hampton Court, 23 road and foot bridges span the Thames, many of them within a few hundred yards of each other. Until 1730, London Bridge was the only route across the river below Kingston-upon-Thames, and there was intense opposition from the City of London when it was suggested that a further bridge should be built at Putney. However, one was finally built there in 1730.

Some 10,000 tons of relatively modern history is firmly anchored offshore between London Bridge and Tower Bridge – H.M.S. *Belfast*, the only major British warship of World War II still afloat. It is a sobering thought to realize that a warship less than 40 years old is now only useful as a museum. She is, in fact, as important a representative of her times as H.M.S. *Victory* is of the Napoleonic wars.

Below Tower Bridge, beyond the Pool of London, dockland, once the busiest port in the world, now seems sadly inactive as shipping finds more seaward ports more convenient. The scenery is flattish, enlivened here and there by an ancient pub, like the Prospect of Whitby, or a handsome riverside church. But like all good theatrical impresarios, Father Thames keeps his big number for the grand finale – the magnificent spectacle of Greenwich. Henry VIII was born here in the Placentia Palace which has long since disappeared. What the visitor sees is a combined operation by several architects over a number of years: Christopher Wren, Nicholas Hawksmoor, John Webb, James Stewart and John Vanbrugh. Between them they built the Greenwich Hospital, now the Royal Naval College. Inigo Jones designed the delightful Queen's House, built in 1616 for Anne of Denmark, James I's queen. She died three years later and the house was finally completed for Henrietta Maria by Charles I. It was added to by John Webb in 1662. The College, the Queen's House, the National Maritime Museum, the Cutty Sark and Gypsy Moth, all of which front the Thames at Greenwich, add up to the most enthralling down-Thames expedition from London it is possible to imagine.

But for the Thames, there would be no London: a fact of life that outsiders have quickly had to learn. When King James I, fresh from Scotland demanded that the City of London should lend him £20,000, the then Lord Mayor told him that they could not. 'Then I will compel you to,' said the king. 'Sire,' said the mayor firmly, 'neither you nor anyone can compel us.' To which the king retorted angrily, 'Then I'll ruin you and your city for ever. I'll remove my courts of law, my court itself and my parliament to Winchester or Oxford and make a desert of Westminster; and then what will become of you?' The Lord Mayor replied quietly, 'May it please your majesty, you are at liberty to remove yourself and your courts wherever you please; but, sire, there will always be one consolation to the merchants of London: your majesty cannot take the Thames with you 〜

IN accordance with a 600 year old tradition, all the swans on the Thames belong either to the Sovereign or to the Vintners or the Dyers, two of the City's livery companies. Each July, teams under three Swan Herdsmen set off on a week's trip up as far as Henley to catch, identify and mark their respective birds, except for those of the Sovereign, which are left unmarked. The expedition is known as Swan Upping. (*Right*)

THE attraction of rowing – the hard, back-aching, muscle-torturing kind – is a mystery to most people, but the Thames at Hammersmith on any Sunday morning demonstrates the hold the sport has on many hundreds of Londoners. The Head of the River Race, usually in March, in which as many as a hundred rowing eights may compete, is far more spectacular than the Oxford and Cambridge Boat Race. (*Below*)

THE Thames at Hammersmith Bridge (*below*) and beneath the towering chimneys of Battersea Power Station (*right*), lies limpid in the thin morning light. But this same familiar, softly flowing river has been – and could be again – an unpredictable menace to the safety of much of London.

'There was last night' wrote Samuel Pepys in his diary for 7 December 1663, 'the greatest tide that ever was remembered in England to have been in this river all Whitehall having been drowned.' And there are records of disastrous Thames floods as far back as 1236 when 'in the great Palace of Westminster men did row with wherries in the midst of the hall.' All long ago! Yes, but not so long ago, in 1928, an exceptionally high tide rose above the embankment parapets, flooded parts of central London and drowned 14 people. Again in 1953 when there was terrible flooding along the east coast and in the Thames Estuary resulting in the loss of 300 lives, London escaped only by the narrowest margin.

Since then banks have again been raised but the threat remains: tides are rising faster than the defences – by over 600mm (2 feet) at London Bridge in the past 100 years. A high Spring tide, flooding down the east coast, spurred on by a following wind, could surge up the Thames Estuary and pour over the existing embankments, paralysing the underground railways, cutting off telephones, gas and electricity, flooding streets, homes and offices and drowning the Londoners in their beds.

The solution to this ever-growing problem that the Greater London Council has adopted is bold, imaginative and – inevitably – costly. Opposite Silvertown in the Woolwich Reach, a gigantic movable flood barrier is being constructed. Pivoted gates that normally lie flat on the river bed, can be swung through 90° to form a continuous steel wall across the river to stem the surge. Once this barrier has been completed, the Thames should be safe at last.

Tower Bridge, symbol of London, silhouetted against the silver Thames. The two central sections, each weighing about 1,000 tonnes, can be raised to allow large vessels to pass further up the river. Bells are rung when this operation is about to happen, which is usually two or three times a day. The bridge was opened in 1894. (*Previous pages*)

Moored opposite the Tower of London, just upstream from Tower Bridge, is the only surviving major warship of World War II – H.M.S. *Belfast*, built in 1939 at the famous Harland & Wolff yard in Belfast, due to be scrapped after 30 years active service, but saved by the H.M.S. *Belfast* Trust which stepped in to buy her for the nation.

Today she is a floating museum, preserving as far as possible the working atmosphere of a ship that took part in the sinking of the *Scharnhorst* off the North Cape of Norway, bombarded the D-Day beaches of Normandy, served in Korean waters and was finally the flagship of Britain's Far Eastern fleet. Her last captain, Rear Admiral Morgan Giles, was also the first chairman of the trust that has saved her from the scrap yard. (*Right*)

THE Thames below Tower Bridge was once a wholly working river and most of the Port of London's trade was waterborne in Thames lighters: clumsy, double-ended, tarpaulin-covered craft here seen swinging at a mooring buoy in the tideway. Changes in ships and cargo-handling methods have made the lighter almost redundant though they are still to be seen either being towed or making skilful use of the tides, loaded with coal for the power stations or timber to be carried to up-river wharves. Thames lighters are 36.6m (120 feet) long and 5.2m (17 feet) wide. (*Left*)

IN 1870, it was estimated, London contained 100,000 tramps, 30,000 paupers, 16,000 criminals and 20,000 public houses – one for every 150 men,

women and children in the city. Right through Queen Victoria's reign, widely regarded as a period of prosperity and propriety, poverty and drunkenness were the twin cankers of working-class society. The London pubs, disparagingly known as gin palaces, had a most unwholesome reputation, not only for drunken debauchery but also as the haunts of criminals and every kind of vice. In the Thameside area of Wapping High Street alone there were 36 public houses and taverns with names such as *North American Sailor*, *Ship and Punchbowl* and *Prospect of Whitby*. Smuggling was their undercover trade and most of them were forced to close, but the *Prospect of Whitby* has survived and become eminently respectable. (*Above*)

THIS vista of Thames-side architecture seen from the Southwark side of London Bridge emphasizes the extraordinary diversity of styles that go into the making of the London scene. One hundred years separate the two buildings on the bridge approach. On the right is the mausoleum-like colossus of Adelaide House, an office block of the 1920s and a style-setter in its day. On the left is the livery hall of the Fishmongers' Company, built in the grand classic manner in 1834. Beyond, is the tower block of the headquarters of the National Westminster Bank, now completed. It is the tallest building in the City. To the left of the picture is a motley collection of boxy buildings that serve their purposes without adding much distinction to London's skyline. The paddle-steamer is a refugee from the Clyde. (*Above*)

FIVE miles downstream from London Bridge the Thames launches tie up at Greenwich, the architectural jewel of riverside London. Through these massive gates topped by a naval crown can be seen the charming villa-like house that James I commissioned Inigo Jones to build for his queen, Anne of Denmark. She died before it was completed and the building was neglected for ten years until Charles I had it completed for Henrietta Maria. On either side, the domes of Greenwich Hospital (later to become the Royal Naval College) record Charles II's ambition to build a worthy replacement for the rambling brick Placentia Palace where Henry VIII was born. William and Mary, preferring to live at Hampton Court, commissioned Sir Christopher

Wren to expand it into an impressive naval hospital, the equivalent of Charles' hospital for soldiers at Chelsea. In 1873 'the most stately procession of buildings we possess' finally became the Royal Naval College. (*Above*)

TWO Thames sailing barges, once busy coastal traders, now mainly privately owned pleasure boats, pass Greenwich in the annual barge race. (*Right*)

THE SOUTH BANK

CENTRAL LONDON SOUTH OF THE THAMES, the strip lying between Vauxhall Bridge and Tower Bridge, has come to be known as South Bank. Tourists observe it from the opposite side of the river but do not often visit it except when they cross to the Festival Hall or the new National Theatre. In addition to its known attractions it contains some evocative glimpses of old London – gaunt warehouses and idle wharves, streets of Dickensian gloom alternating with rows of squat, friendly homes.

South Bank isn't a place in the accepted sense of the word yet it has a strong sense of community. Hundreds of years of being on the 'wrong side of the river' has bred in its people a cheerful pugnacity that is the mark of the south Londoner. They know that Lambeth and Camberwell have little in common with Mayfair and Marylebone, but they know to which they would rather belong.

Near the eastern end of Lambeth Bridge, the brick gateway built by Archbishop Morton in 1495 marks the entrance to Lambeth Palace, the London home of Archbishops of Canterbury for close on 800 years. The extent of the Palace and its grounds indicate the almost regal splendour in which earlier archbishops lived, with their private armies and shoals of retainers – in marked contrast to the comparative austerity of the present archbishop's household. The Palace, severely damaged in the London *Blitz*, has been carefully restored but, sadly, is no longer open to the public because of staffing problems.

Southwark, which surrounds the southern approach to London Bridge, was the first area of development south of the river. Beyond it were scattered villages, mere country cousins, some with an excellent view of the growing city across the water.

In parkland, quite close to London Bridge, was the Bishop of Winchester's 13th century palace. It was long thought to have disappeared but a stone wall of it containing a rose window was recently revealed when a warehouse was being demolished. By the end of the 16th century the bishop had become landlord of much of the property surrounding his palace. The area, known as the Liberty of the Clink – a term used for those areas outside the jurisdiction of the City of London – became infested with brothels, low taverns and bull- and bear-baiting rings,

most of which paid rent to the bishop. Queen Elizabeth I used to come here to the Paris Garden with the French ambassadors to enjoy the animal-baiting.

Playhouses were not permitted in the City of London, so Bankside saw the establishment of London's first theatres and here Shakespeare lived and worked. He had a ten per cent interest in the Globe Playhouse which was burnt to the ground in 1613, but by then Shakespeare had returned to Stratford-upon-Avon and was not financially involved in the loss.

There is a tradition that Sir Christopher Wren lived in a house on Bankside when St Paul's Cathedral was being built after its destruction in the fire of 1666. If the tradition is true, Cardinal's Wharf, a house that is claimed to have been his, was in an ideal position as it would have given Wren a wide and uninterrupted view of his work. It is a pleasant 17th century house next door to that of the Provost of Southwark Cathedral.

Southwark Cathedral's square, pinnacled tower is a famous landmark in south-east London. It began life as the Priory of St Mary Overie – meaning 'over the river'. After the dissolution of the monasteries it served as Southwark's parish church and was renamed St Saviour's. It was made a cathedral with the double dedication of St Saviour and St Mary Overie only in 1905. Though architecturally very mixed, it is a building of considerable charm and character, qualities emphasized by its rather drab surroundings. There is not much of the early church

LONDON'S South Bank shuffles every card in the architectural pack from the aggressive concrete parapets of the Festival Hall complex to the faded Victorian brickwork façades of deserted riverside warehouses. The Thames, in the centre of London, turns through a complete right-angle totally confusing most people's sense of direction. St Paul's Cathedral, which here seems to be so much part of the picture, is in fact on the north bank of the river. (*Right*)

THE sombre concrete architecture of the Royal Festival Hall's riverside frontage is here just visible, enlivened by the gaily coloured flags and decorations. (*Above*)

left that can be dated with assurance. Fragments of the Norman building survive in the north transept, and the south transept is genuine 14th century, but much of the building dates from the two major restorations of 1838 and 1890. There is the inevitable memorial to William Shakespeare (he was buried, of course, at Stratford-upon-Avon) and also to his lesser known brother Edmund, an actor who died at the early age of 27 and is buried beneath the choir. The Harvard Chapel, rebuilt in 1907, commemorates John Harvard, the founder of Harvard University.

Moving upstream, just before Waterloo Bridge, one is confronted by the all too solid concrete hull of the new National Theatre. This monument to persistence had its foundation stone laid in Kensington more than 50 years ago. Like the Flying Dutchman it seemed doomed to sail in limbo until, largely thanks to the Greater London Council who donated the site, it finally made harbour beside the Thames. And what a splendid ship it has turned out to be with its

three auditoriums and its totally new attitude to theatre-going. Instead of merely coming to the theatre, watching the performance and going home again, the National Theatre audience is invited to come early and stay late; wander around the lushly-carpeted complex; eat and drink on the terraces or in the foyers; enter into discussions with the actors; be entertained by strolling musicians and pop groups; and generally become part of the show. It seems to be an attitude that is working well and one that should greatly contribute to the South Bank resurgence in spite of the theatre's lofty, tower-block neighbour, London Weekend Television, whose aim must surely be to keep the folks at home.

The South Bank resurgence really dates back to the decision to hold the 1951 Festival of Britain (celebrating the centenary of the famous 1851 Exhibition) on what was virtually derelict land between Waterloo Bridge and County Hall. As its contribution to the Festival, the then London County Council (now Greater London

Council) built the Royal Festival Hall, an object of much controversy in its day, but now acknowledged as a landmark in London's postwar architecture and a triumph of internal planning and acoustic engineering. In the nearly 30 years since its opening, the Royal Festival Hall has provided Londoners – and millions of London visitors – with a rich musical diet.

Between the Royal Festival Hall and Waterloo Bridge a further concrete complex has taken what some people might describe as shape: the Queen Elizabeth Hall for smaller concerts (the Royal Festival Hall seats 3,000), the Purcell Room for recitals and the Hayward Gallery where a series of exhibitions is arranged by the Arts Council of Great Britain. In spite of their austere exteriors, all these buildings are warm, comfortable and even beautiful within.

To celebrate Queen Elizabeth II's 1977 Silver Jubilee, most of the vacant land between the Royal Festival Hall and County Hall has been transformed into an imaginative garden with play space for children.

REDEVELOPMENT on the South Bank has produced some impressive buildings including (on the right of the picture) the new National Theatre and the London Weekend Television Centre. Waterloo Bridge, in the foreground, completed in 1939 but not officially opened until 1945, is generally considered to be London's most handsome bridge. Beyond it, on the left of the picture, the Union International building combines advertising with architecture, by injecting one of the company's brand names into the decorative detail of the tall tower. (*Left*)

WHEN post-war plans were drawn up for the development of the South Bank, skateboarding was unknown if not undreamt of. The broad concrete terraces and gentle inclines around the Festival Hall have inevitably become the St Moritz of the skateboarding buffs and the balconies provide a safe and excellent viewpoint for the sport's supporters. (*Right*)

LONDON's always impressive and often dramatic sunsets, meeting no resistance from the Thames, fall with especial brilliance on the Royal Festival Hall, London's finest concert hall.

The hall is a success story of civic enterprise if ever there was one. Designed by Sir J. L. Martin and Sir Robert Matthew, the then unknighted resident architects of the Council, it was built as London's contribution to the 1951 Festival of Britain held on the then derelict acres of the South Bank. Ever since it has been run by a manager responsible to a GLC committee, with all the verve and panache of a continental impresario. Nearly all the world's leading artists and orchestras have performed in it. (*Below*)

County Hall, the dominant headquarters of the Greater London Council, is relatively modern. It was designed by Ralph Knott who died four years before the main block was completed in 1933. More blocks have been added since to cope with the increasing size of London and the growing responsibilities of a council whose annual budget amounts to some £2,000 million. To the visitor, the interior of County Hall presents miles of highly polished corridors flanked by regiments of doors. Perhaps the most interesting feature to the outsider is its excellent bookshop where you can buy almost everything that has ever been written, drawn or photographed about London. Outside, at the southern approach to Westminster Bridge, stands the Coade stone lion that had to be evacuated from the Festival of Britain site in 1951. It is not an aggressive beast but it does, perhaps, serve to remind the people of London on the other side of the bridge that much of their welfare is determined by the Greater London Council here on the southern bank.

THERE is a move afoot to release Southwark Cathedral from its dwarfing surroundings and let in light and air to a building whose exterior is worthy of an uncluttered view. Southwark developed around the southern end of the first ever bridge across the Thames and there was a church on the cathedral site in the first years of the 12th century. This Norman church was burned in 1212 and the church built in its stead was one of the first in England to be designed in the new Gothic style. Though the church, in recent centuries, has been insensitively restored, there is an authenticity about its pinnacled tower that validates the whole building. (*Left*)

PRESERVED with care, as befits the last of its kind, the *George Inn*, Southwark is one of the most popular stopping places for organized tours of London; there are not many monuments that serve a pint of beer to the onlooker. The inn's uniqueness is its galleried courtyard where the coaches from Dover and Canterbury would stop to set down their passengers and change horses. Built in 1676 after a great fire had destroyed much of Southwark, a large part of the original inn was demolished in 1889. (*Right*)

THIS fine Tudor gateway, built by Cardinal Morton in 1490 is, apart from a glimpse of the Lollards' Tower, about as much of Lambeth Palace as most Londoners ever see. But once through its formidable doorway an absolute revelation of spaciousness opens up to the visitor. As a home, it greatly over-provides for the present Archbishop's modest needs. But it is also the office of the man who is Bishop of the Diocese of Canterbury, Archbishop of the Southern Province, Primate of All England, Chairman of the Church Assembly and head of the world-wide Anglican Communion. It is in the administration of all these important offices that full use is made of the Palace's many buildings, ancient and modern. (*Right*)

COCKNEY LONDON – THE EAST END

THE CHURCH OF ST MARY-LE-BOW IN Cheapside is one of Sir Christopher Wren's most splendid churches – especially the pinnacled square tower supporting the pillared rotunda with its slender spire. Within this tower hangs a chime of 12 bells including one – the Great Bell of Bow – whose sonorous boom is said to have recalled the young Dick Whittington from Highgate, ultimately to become London's most celebrated Lord Mayor. But there is another legend connected with these bells (they crashed to the floor of the tower during the *Blitz* and have been re-cast from the original metal) and that is the belief that to be a true Cockney you must have been born within their sound. The converse – that everyone born within the sound of Bow Bells is a Cockney – is certainly not true.

The derivation of the word Cockney is obscure, but it has come to be applied to the people of London living mainly to the east of the city – a special kind of person, born and bred of a long line of cheerful, quick witted, gregarious, independent people who have lived hard and laboured hard in an often inhospitable environment. That most of them happen to live east of St Mary-le-Bow rather than west is a matter of history and, perhaps, of the prevailing wind.

London's East End (in contrast to its fashionable counterpart the West End) does not feature much in the guide books though, to the sociologist, it teems with interest. In the 30 and more years since the end of World War II it has experienced probably more – and certainly more fundamental – changes than any other part of London.

Sadly the London costermongers are a dying race, for it is they who have always been the core of Cockney London. In the 19th century this irrepressible band of highly independent, mobile traders was said to number nearly 40,000. Nothing but their tough, cynical good humour and grim determination (as the *Blitz* was later to prove) could have kept them going in face of the grinding poverty and discouragement of life in the East End of those times. They lived – or, rather, existed – as close as they could to the great London markets and dockland merchants who supplied their stock-in-trade. Their day began with the opening of Smithfield or Billingsgate or Covent Garden long before

dawn when they would load up their barrows for the day's trading. From then on, probably without a proper meal and often until nearly midnight, they would tramp the streets calling their wares and selling in pennyworths to people often poorer than themselves. Sometimes, by the day's end, the coster would find that his takings did not cover the cost of his often perishable stock which he had to dump at a loss. Before he could stock up for the next day he would have to borrow from the moneylender and pay an exorbitant rate of interest. Even in a good week he might earn less than twenty shillings with which to pay the rent and support an inevitably growing family. The pawnbrokers did a roaring trade and, to the mortification of the reformers, so did the pubs.

But Cockney optimism persisted – as their taste in amusements demonstrated: the singing in the pubs; the robust music halls (there were 400 in London alone at the end of the 19th century); the boisterous bank holiday outings to Hampstead Heath, Epping Forest or the Crystal Palace; the occasional day trip to the seaside; the rare working holiday hop-picking in Kent.

Cockneys are a gregarious people and, as such, they were extremely tolerant of the immigrants from the north of England, from Ireland and from Europe at a time when London was expanding at a dizzy pace. The construction of the London docks, the railway termini, roads, houses, waterworks and sewage systems brought unskilled labourers and the unemployed flooding into the eastern suburbs in their thousands. Writing of the docks in the 1850s, Henry Mayhew, whose book *London Labour and the London Poor* is a classic of its kind, said:

> Those persons who are unable to live by the occupation to which they have been educated can obtain a living there without any previous training. Hence we find men of every calling labouring at the docks. There are decayed and bankrupt master butchers, master bakers, publicans, grocers, old soldiers, old sailors, Polish refugees, broken-down gentlemen, discharged lawyers' clerks, suspended government clerks, almsmen, pensioners, servants, thieves – indeed everyone who wants a loaf and is prepared to work for it.

'Working for it' brought them in perhaps four-

pence an hour and even that depended upon the wind being in the right quarter to enable shipping to sail up the estuary.

Their homes were mostly rudimentary hovels, but the demand produced a supply of cheap, simple terraced houses spreading over the flat and sometimes marshy landscape of Stepney, Poplar, Mile End, Stratford and Bow. Living was inevitably a communal affair but that suited the Cockney temperament. Everyone knew his neighbour. Help was always close at hand in an emergency.

Out of these close-knit communities grew an organization that is known perhaps more widely overseas than it is in the rest of Britain –

the Pearlies who epitomize the generous Cockney spirit. It was begun by a small band of public-spirited costermongers anxious to alleviate the tragic poverty they saw around them but who realized that they could expect help from no-one but themselves.

The familiar all-over pearly dress is said to have been first worn by a roadsweeper named Henry Croft who used to help a group of coster-mongers in their charitable work. Pearl buttons were the fashionable dress accessory of the period and Croft created something of a sensation when he appeared in the ultimate all-button outfit in one of the charity carnival processions. The fashion spread to other parts of London and it

became the custom to select a 'pearly' leader in each borough. The leadership became an heredi-tary office handed down from father to son – the Pearly Kings and Queens of London. To see them in their splendour, visit the church of St Martin-in-the-Fields on the first Sunday in October for the annual Pearly Harvest Festival. It is unique.

Great changes came to the East End in the aftermath of World War II. Whole streets had been wiped out by enemy bombing and, in an effort to economize on land, tower blocks of flats were built to rehouse the very overcrowded population. Cockneys soon discovered that this new vertical living had none of the advantages of

THE Victorian age still lingers on in many aspects of Cockney London, and particularly in its pubs – in this case the *White Hart* in Mile End Road. The Victorian pub has come right back into fashion and those owners who have been wise enough not to modernize their decor find that their mahogany bars and engraved mirrors are now collectors pieces. But quite apart from its furnishings, the East End pub – old or new – is one of the friendliest (if noisiest) places on earth. (*Below*)

the horizontal system they were accustomed to before: no sitting at the door and chatting on a summer's evening; no friends to call to across the street; no opportunity to observe the comings and goings of the day; no way of keeping an eye on the children at play; no meeting and nattering in the corner shop. All these had been the small change of living that made up for some of the hardships of life. Now they were all gone and only a distant view of London from a fourteenth-floor balcony was offered instead. The warmth and humanity of Cockney street life was something the planners had overlooked.

It is difficult for the tourist to acquire the flavour of the East End. Emerging from the underground at Whitechapel or taking a bus to Wapping, he will find little to attract his eye other than the picturesque riverside pubs like the Prospect of Whitby, a smartened-up smugglers' inn, or the unexpectedly avant-garde exhibitions at the Whitechapel Art Gallery. In Stepney there are some splendid, outsize churches by that master-architect Nicholas Hawksmoor – St Anne, Limehouse, Christ Church, Spitalfields and St George-in-the-East, Cannon Street Road.

The area around St Katherine's Dock gives perhaps the best and most hopeful picture of what the future of the East End could be. Here, just east of the Tower of London, the run-down dock area has been imaginatively transformed in a joint operation by the Greater London Council and the Taylor Woodrow Property Company. The disused dock is now a yacht haven with sleek and expensive cruisers moored close to brown-sailed Thames barges and the retired Trinity House lightship from the Nore. A large and luxurious hotel looks out towards Tower Bridge while behind the yacht haven is the rather grandiosely named World Trade Centre which turns out to be a block of modern office suites with centralized communication and secretarial services. Around the yacht haven are restaurants, pubs and shops and, to the east and on the river bank, a well planned housing estate of some seven hundred dwellings, of which nearly half will be occupied by GLC tenants.

If all of London's near-derelict dockland could be given an equally imaginative (but inevitably expensive) face-lift, what a pleasing place much of London's East End could become 🌿🐾

EAST London, poor as many of its inhabitants used to be, was not all slums and hovels. Tredegar Square, the south side of which is seen through some of London's ubiquitous plane trees, was built in 1835 to house what would be known today as the managerial class. By the 1880s these houses, handsome as they still are, were beginning to lose their middle class tenants and today they are mainly divided into flats, though the district, like Islington, is tending to become fashionable once again with young couples looking for homes of character. (*Left*)

WAPPING, thanks to authors like Charles Dickens, Sax Rhomer and Edgar Wallace, has a sinister sound. Here in their novels you find bodies floating in the Thames, heroes trapped in flooded basements, and opium dens and smugglers' hideouts in every deserted warehouse. You must use a lot of imagination to make Wapping seem like that today. Between the under-used Thames and the destitute docks, Wapping is a grey, rather sad

shadow of what was once a rumbustious, sea-going hamlet with more pubs per person than any other part of London. Its pubs – the *Prospect of Whitby* is one of them – are still warm, welcoming, cheerful and flourishing. (*Below left*)

ST Katherine's is the first of the disused London docks to be given a facelift. The Ivory House, a former warehouse, has been converted into a row of tourist-attracting shops, with offices and apartments above. The old dock basin which used to house salt-caked cargo ships is now the mooring place for smart yachts and cruisers. (*Below*)

The deep charitable instincts of London's
Cockneys express themselves in an organization
that flourishes more strongly south of the Thames
than north – the Pearlies. The Pearly Kings and
Queens – the royal families of Cockneydom –
usually inherit their titles from their fathers and
mothers, but the obligation that goes with the title
is to engage in charitable activities, raising money
for good causes and seeing that no fellow Cockney is
in need. Mindful of their blessings, the Pearlies hold
an annual Costermongers' Harvest Festival. Before
the war this service took place in the church of
St Mary Magdalene in Congreve Street off the Old
Kent Road, but the church was destroyed in an air
raid and the service has been transferred to St
Martin-in-the-Fields, the famous church on the
corner of Trafalgar Square.
The scene outside St Martin's after the service
shows to what lengths the Pearlies go to elaborate
their outfits. Coats, skirts and trousers are em-
blazoned with hundreds of pearl buttons, and hats
are adorned with gaily coloured ostrich plumes –
sartorial extroversion at its most pungent. (*Left*)

One of the landmarks of East London is Tubby
Isaac's jellied eel stall in Goulston Street off
Aldgate High Street. To visit London without
sampling Tubby's jellied eels is like failing to try
clam chowder in New England or curry in India.
In Victorian times there were more than five hundred
such stalls scattered over East London. Casual
labourers, many of them unmarried and without
homes of their own, had nowhere else to eat. Tastes
may change but Tubby is unlikely to go out of
business while Cockneys are still around. (*Below*)

LIVING in the East End has always been cramped so the Cockney doesn't waste space. His backyard is often a miracle of compressed utility, and when it comes to business, what's wrong with railway arches? (*Right*)

ANOTHER relic of a bygone age still lingers on in the East End. The rag and bone man, who may equally be an 'any-old-iron' man, spreads his net wide, working the inner suburbs or, as here, 'up west'. He performs a useful service for the London housewife, taking away old mangles or worn out gas fires that are otherwise hard to dispose of. He is a shrewd buyer and there are few objects that he can't find a market for. (*Above*)

BILLINGSGATE, London's fish market, is a Cockney island that has strayed into the City. It is certainly beside the river which, in centuries past, provided much of its fish, but its character is at odds with the banks and bowlers to the north. Myriad glazed-eyed fish lie on slabs and in boxes while their virtues are proclaimed at full volume to the fishmongers and restaurateurs who have risen before dawn to get the best choice. It is a cold but cheerful place with earthy language and watery floors, and anyone who wants to see, hear and smell Billingsgate at its best must get there early too. The Market is named after a river gate in the City wall which has long ago disappeared. (*Far right*)

OUTER &
RURAL LONDON

THE ROMANS WERE RIGHT IF THEY JUDGED that the wall they built around London would fix its boundaries for a thousand years, for it was not until early medieval times that sheer pressure from within forced the growth of settlements outside the wall, and with the bridging of the Thames in the 10th century, London's remaining boundary to the south was breached if not abolished.

As students of Parkinson's Law well know, where there is room for expansion, expansion takes place. So, in the next thousand years of its life, London expanded, slowly at first, but at what we now see was an accelerating pace. The one square mile known as The City has grown into the more than 600 square miles known as Greater London. Six hundred square miles – four hundred thousand acres – one hundred and sixty thousand hectares – however it is expressed, London covers an immense amount of land. From Charing Cross it is possible to travel more than 20 km (12 miles) in any direction and still be within the confines of Greater London. In recent years parts of Kent, Surrey, Hertfordshire and Essex and the whole of Middlesex have been sucked into 'the great wen of all' as William Cobbett contemptuously called London in his lifelong crusade against the outward spread of the city. Recent growth has created obvious absurdities: the transfer of Kingston-upon-Thames into Greater London, for instance, means that Surrey's county hall is no longer in Surrey.

Even 15 years ago it would have been unthinkable to speak of someone living in, say, Northwood or Coulsdon as a Londoner, but that's what they are today, as are the people of Bromley, Barnet, Croydon and Harrow. But William Cobbett can rest in peace: the limits of London have now been fixed: the so-called 'green belt' that surrounds it is (so the politicians

assure us) inviolable. Even those who hold that big is beautiful now agree that London is big enough. During its lifelong foraging expeditions London has devoured dozens of separate small towns and villages. Most of those near the heart of London have been under the city's domination for so long that they have become suburbanized and lost their individuality. Two notable exceptions to this generalization are Hampstead and Dulwich, one a few miles north of the City, the other a similar distance south.

Long before Hampstead became a part of London, wealthy Londoners took to its breezy uplands for the sake of their families' health. In the early part of the 19th century, when Sir Thomas Wilson was Lord of the Manor of Hampstead, a public inquiry revealed that he regarded the heath as his private property and that he was negotiating to sell it as building land for £2½ million. Fortunately the law concerned with common land rights prevented him from doing so and, in 1872, his successor was quite glad to dispose of it for £55,045 to the Metropolitan Board of Works, forerunner to the Greater London Council, who guaranteed public access for all time.

Dulwich owes its preservation to Edward Alleyn, an actor-manager and contemporary of Shakespeare who, in 1605, bought the Manor of Dulwich for £10,000. It was a lot of money for even a successful actor-manager to put his hand on in those days, but as some 600 hectares (1,500 acres) of land went with the manorial rights, it was something of a bargain. Fortunately for Dulwich, most of the land is still intact. In 1616 Alleyn founded the College of God's Gift from which sprang Dulwich College, Alleyn's School, the almshouses and chapel, and the Dulwich College Picture Gallery, one of the finest collections of pictures outside central London. Dulwich Park (now the responsibility

KENWOOD House, surrounded by its lake and 80 hectares (200 acres) of landscaped grounds, was re-built for the first Earl of Mansfield in 1767 by Robert Adam. A later owner, Lord Iveagh, who died in 1927, bequeathed it to the nation together with the furniture and his fabulous collection of pictures including works by Rembrandt, Gainsborough, Vermeer, Franz Hals, Reynolds, Raeburn and Van Dyck. Its extensive grounds adjoin Hampstead Heath. (*Left*)

of the Greater London Council) was 'presented to the people of London' and opened by Lord Rosebery in 1890. An observer writing about Dulwich over 100 years ago wrote that 'the craving of merchants for suburban residences has done much to alter the aspect of the place but, compared with neighbouring suburbs, it has died hard and not until William Cowper's "opulent, enlarged and still-increasing London" has laid its hands upon it, will Dulwich surrender its individuality'. Dulwich has evidently continued to die very hard for its individuality remains unsurrendered.

Close to Dulwich is another of London's lungs – the Crystal Palace, a name which must puzzle those who do not know its historical significance. When the Great Exhibition of 1851 closed, its main exhibition hall, a unique structure of cast iron and glass designed by Sir Joseph Paxton, was moved from Hyde Park to the

slopes of Sydenham and re-erected in a newly created park. It was opened by Queen Victoria in 1854 and became a highly popular centre for entertainment throughout south London and universally known as the Crystal Palace. The building was severely damaged by fire in 1866 and totally destroyed 70 years later in the most spectacular blaze London had seen since the Palace of Westminster fire in 1834. The Crystal Palace park now contains a children's zoo and, beside the lake, a collection of life-size, prehistoric monsters carved in 1853. Part of the park has been given over to the National Sports Centre, one of the best equipped sports stadiums and training centres in Europe.

Thirteen km (eight miles) to the south-east, beyond Bromley, there is a large area of totally rural countryside unaffected by its allegiance to London. In its centre is the village of Downe where Charles Darwin, the scientist, came to live

after his marriage to his cousin, Emma Wedgwood, and where he died in 1882. Wild life is to be expected in such unspoilt surroundings, but it is surprising how much and how varied is the wild life much closer to London's centre. The parks are natural habitats for many varieties of birds, but less common breeds, like owls, kestrels and peregrine falcons heve been observed in central London, and a pair of black redstarts is known to have raised young in the precincts of Westminster Abbey. The outer suburbs with their stretches of heath and common, their sometimes overgrown cemeteries and their larger gardens attract birds that are familiar throughout southern England, while lakes, reservoirs and flooded gravel pits provide sanctuary for an astonishing variety of water-fowl – teal, wigeon, common pochard, tufted duck, goosander, great crested grebe and coot among them.

Both Bushey Park and Richmond Park have

THOMAS Gibson, a President in the Board of Trade in the reign of George IV, developed the square in Islington that is named after him. Two identical terraces, built about 1832, face each other across formal gardens. The neo-classical gazebo in the gardens is a sham – it screens a ventilating shaft for the Underground. (*Right*)

NIKOLAUS Pevsner, the doyen of architectural critics, considers Church Row to be the best street in Hampstead – praise indeed because Hampstead is very rich in architectural pleasures. The houses on the south side of the Row, leading to the Parish Church, were built about 1720. Those on the north side are slightly earlier, smaller and more varied. (*Far right*)

large herds of deer, but wild deer from Kent, Surrey and Hertfordshire often wander across the boundaries into London without asking the Lord Mayor's permission. But then the Lord Mayor has his own herd of deer in Epping Forest, most of which is not in London at all. In 1882 the City Corporation, with commendable foresight, bought 2,500 hectares (6,000 acres) of the forest for £250,000 for the benefit of the people of London. To give west Londoners equal opportunity to enjoy a day in the country, the Corporation also bought Burnham Beeches, the lovely wooded area near Slough.

Richmond Park, in addition to its herd of deer, has badgers, hares, foxes, rabbits and weasels living in the wild only ten km (six miles) from Westminster.

In several areas on the outskirts of London country parks are being developed for sport and recreation. Two are at Trent Park, Enfield and

in Hainault Forest, adjoining the London boundary near Chigwell. To the west of London, the valley of the river Colne is to become a regional park where sailing, fishing and riding will be catered for.

Throughout London, there are excellent opportunities in parks and public gardens to study – or merely admire – plants and flowers of every kind. The Royal Botanic Gardens, Kew, is world-renowned for its collection but, on the opposite bank of the Thames, at Syon House, home of the Duke of Northumberland, plants can be both admired and bought. In the grounds of this historic house, with its superb rose-garden and collection of fuchsias, there is a garden centre where it is possible to buy everything the ardent gardener could desire. Not very far away, in Richmond Park, the Isabella Plantation puts on a dazzling show of dwarf azaleas and rhododendrons in springtime.

There is so much going on in outer London that the five millions who live there find less and less need to come into central London for their entertainment. Bromley, for example, has recently opened its new Churchill Theatre. Richmond and Greenwich have lively theatres of their own. The Fairfield Halls in Croydon's city-like centre welcome most of Europe's finest conductors and their orchestras. You can ice skate at Streatham and Twickenham or roller skate at the Alexandra Palace. Wimbledon and tennis are synonymous. Wembley Stadium has staged both the Olympic games and the World Cup. Open-air concerts are held beside the lake at Kenwood House and at the Crystal Palace Concert Bowl. A quarter of a million people join adult education classes throughout Greater London.

One way and another the outer Londoner need never have a dull moment 🍃🐦

THOUGH most of Epping Forest is outside the boundary of London, it does in fact belong to London, having been bought by the City Corporation for the benefit of Londoners and opened to the public in 1882. Today's forest is only a fraction of its original size but even so it extends to 2500 hectares (6000 acres) of almost untamed woodland – an unassailable stretch of London's Green Belt. The Corporation paid £250,000 for the forest and, although there was opposition to the expenditure at the time, hindsight proves that, for once at least, the ratepayers got good value. (*Left*)

THIS view of Syon House from across the lake in Kew Gardens disguises the fact that the River Thames flows between them. Before local government reorganization, Syon House was in Middlesex, and Kew was in Surrey; now both are for administrative purposes in London. The somewhat austere battlemented building is crowned by the stiff-tailed lion emblem of the Percys, the family name of the Duke of Northumberland whose home it is. This particular lion came from no further away than central London – it was on Northumberland House, demolished in 1874 to make room for Northumberland Avenue. Within the house there is a wealth of treasures ranging from the grandeur of Robert Adam's Great Hall to the gnarled oak stake, believed to have been part of a palisade erected here on the north side of the Thames by the ancient Britons in an attempt to prevent Julius Caesar and his legions from crossing the river.

Syon began life as a monastery but because of 'the Incontynensye of the Nunnes of Syon with the Friores' Henry VIII did not have to search for excuses to dissolve it and transfer it to the Crown. He kept Catherine Howard prisoner at Syon prior to her execution in 1542, and five years later his own body rested here overnight on its way to burial at Windsor.

Twenty-three hectares (55 acres) of splendid grounds surround Syon House, laid out by 'Capability' Brown who planted many of the superb cedars, limes, oaks and chestnuts. The Great Conservatory was the work of Charles Fowler who later was to build the iron and glass halls of Covent Garden market. It is said that Joseph Paxton made a very thorough examination of the conservatory before designing the Crystal Palace 20 years later. In 1965 the 10th Duke in collaboration with I.C.I. founded the Gardening Centre that occupies part of the grounds. (*Above*)

FOOTBALL – the soccer variety – is big business in and around London where there are a dozen clubs with teams in one or other division of the Football League. Most of the grounds are in built-up areas which means that they occupy valuable and heavily-rated land that is only profitably employed about one day a week. Financial pressure is forcing some clubs to consider sharing their grounds with neighbouring clubs in an effort to make ends meet. The photograph shows Queens Park Rangers playing a home match on their ground at Loftus Road, Shepherd's Bush. The finals of the Football Association Cup and the League Cup are always played in the Wembley Stadium which can accommodate about 100,000 spectators. (*Below*)

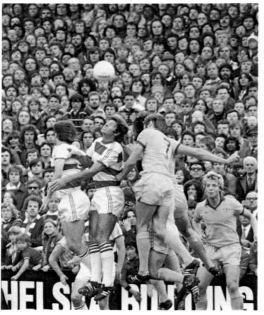

SPORT of a much more genteel character is enjoyed at the Hurlingham Club, an oasis of green beside the Thames near Putney Bridge. Polo was played here up to 1939, but activities are now limited to tennis, swimming, croquet, squash and bowls. Hurlingham is a strongly social club famous for its annual pre-Wimbledon garden party at which most of the tournament's star players may be seen. An old guide to London suggests that the name Hurlingham derives from the ancient sport of hurling. 'It is now best known' the guide continues, 'for its grounds, which are much patronised by the lovers of pigeon-shooting and other aristocratic pastimes of a similar character'. (*Right*)

Boys' Public Schools in Britain are usually large, always independent, sometimes very ancient. There are some twenty in London of which the best known are Harrow in north London, Westminster in central London and Dulwich in south London. The earliest of these three, Westminster, was founded in 1566. Harrow followed in 1571 and Dulwich, a comparative newcomer, in 1619. On 21 June that year James I signed the document which permitted Edward Alleyn, an actor contemporary of Shakespeare, to establish the College of God's Gift, the trust which now administers Dulwich College, several other schools and charities and the Dulwich College Picture Gallery. Dulwich College soon outgrew its 17th century home and in 1866 the extensive school buildings seen in the photograph were designed by Charles Barry, son of Sir Charles Barry, the architect of the Houses of Parliament. The school today numbers some 1500 boys. Among the Old Alleynians (as the old boys of Dulwich College are called) are Sir Ernest Shackleton, the famous explorer, and Peter Oosterhuis, the equally famous golfer. Another, of course, was P. G. Wodehouse, perhaps the most widely known of them all. (*Left*)

Unlike Syon House which was – and still is – a stately home – Chiswick House, a brilliant example of architectural virtuosity, was built as a meeting place rather than a home. The third Earl of Burlington, who designed it with the technical help of William Kent, had twice done the grand tour of Italy and had fallen under the spell of buildings by Palladio and of their English offspring, those of Inigo Jones.

Chiswick House in later years had a chequered career, at one time becoming the annexe to a mental hospital. It suffered bomb damage but, taken over by the Government, has been most fastidiously restored by the Department of the Environment. The photograph shows the stone stairway leading to the giant portico over the entrance. (*Right*)

These extraordinary animals were sculpted in 1853 to populate the park that had been laid out around the Crystal Palace, brought from its original site – the 1851 Great Exhibition in Hyde Park – to the slopes of Sydenham Hill in South London. The animals are still there, but the Crystal Palace was totally destroyed in a dramatic hill-top fire in 1936. The animals – all extinct – include the Iguanodon, Palaeotherium and Anoplotherium. (*Below*)